On Being Human

VICTOR L. BROWN JR. and REGENIA MOODY CHADWICK

Deseret Book Company Salt Lake City, Utah 1971

Library of Congress No. 71-156813
SBN No. 87747-441-9

Copyright 1971
Deseret Book Company

IN THE UNITED STATES OF AMERICA

Preface and Acknowledgements

This book was written because the authors found that many fine Latter-day Saint parents were deeply concerned about raising their children in today's society, but were confused by the complicated and often conflicting theories advanced by people who were not oriented to the gospel of Jesus Christ. Also, it was found that many parents were seeking complex solutions to basically simple problems.

The authors do not pretend to know all the answers. They do know, however, that the solutions to many human problems are deceptively simple and that the keys to social-emotional health lie in the gospel of Jesus Christ.

This book relates basic principles of human development and mental health to the gospel plan and suggests how problems might be handled within the framework of the Church. This is not a "how to" book on child care. Actual situations, with names and identifying facts changed, are presented to help explain basic principles which parents and other interested people can then apply as needed in varying circumstances.

Bear in mind that while each person is unique and each solution different, if parents can learn true, general principles, they can then generally apply them to the specific situation with which they are concerned.

May we recognize the major contribution Edmund Tucker, our colleague in Nevada, who has put most of these concepts to work with noticeable success. We also wish to acknowledge the fine work of Dorothy Hardy and LaVon Adams who typed the manuscript.

Also, thanks to those who read our early efforts and gave enough encouragement to overcome the inevitable discouragements of attempting this type of venture, especially our editor, Larry Hiller.

Contents

Chapter	Title	Page
1	Social/Emotional Illness and the Scriptures	1
2	Basic Personality—Emotional and Mental Factors "Spirits and Computers"	9
3	Love, the Great Commandment	21
4	The First Year of Life "Infancy: Introduction to Mortality"	33
5	Early Childhood Two Through Four "Trial and Error"	49
6	Middle Childhood: Five Through Seven "Practice Makes Perfect"	69
7	Pre-Adolescence: Eight Through Twelve "The Age of Accountability"	85
8	Adolescence "Adulthood Unrecognized"	103
9	Adulthood "Childhood Revisited"	131
10	The Later Years "Enduring (and Growing) to the End"	159

Chapter 1
Social/Emotional Illness and the Scriptures

Chapter 1

Social/Emotional Illness and the Scriptures

Life today is often a confused affair. Violence, immorality, and fear plague our society. Mankind grows desperate, applying solutions which are often worse than the original problem. In many minds, there is no thought of God as the answer. This is tragic. The simplest way out of the confusion is to follow the Lord's course, which is laid out in the scriptures.

> And I now give unto you a commandment to beware concerning yourselves, to give diligent heed to the words of eternal life.
> For you shall live by every word that proceedeth forth from the mouth of God.
> For the word of the Lord is truth, and whatsoever is truth is light, and whatsoever is light is Spirit, even the Spirit of Jesus Christ. (D&C 84:43-45.)

The human family does not generally see the great, depressing problems of today in proper context. Nuclear terror, wars, famine, pollution, racial strife—all seem to grow out of *social* sickness to which many people attempt to apply grandiose and usually costly cures. They are usually disappointed.

The flaw in this approach is that sick *people* make a sick society. Improvement therefore must start with individuals. In view of this, it would seem that to understand those principles which lead to healthy growth and development—physical, mental, moral, spiritual—ought to be a first priority. And the very first priority must be the home.

Personal trouble is often linked with sin, but people with social or emotional problems (which includes nearly everyone at some time in his life) are not necessarily sinners. Some have sinned, of course, and some are the victims of sin. Many, however, are ignorant in the sense that they literally do not know what to do to be stable and happy. Even those who understand their problems sometimes cannot, or do not, do what is necessary to overcome them. They are not free in the scriptural sense that "the truth shall make you free." (John 8:32.)

The scriptures also state that, "The glory of God is intelligence, or, in other words, light and truth." (D&C 93:36.) This can also mean that God, being perfectly intelligent, is perfectly well mentally. He is stable, happy, peaceful. The more godlike man becomes, the less vulnerable he is to social or emotional illness. And, the more godly a society, the healthier it becomes.

These statements are made with one reservation, however—that people must go about their tasks according to the Lord's plan. Again this is stated very well in the scriptures.

I, the Lord, stretched out the heavens, and built the earth, my very handiwork; and all things therein are mine.

And it is my purpose to provide for my saints, for all things are mine.

But it must needs be done in mine own way.... (D&C 104:14-16.)

In dealing with all these problems, our society has become accustomed to complicated, expensive programs that do not always resemble the Lord's way. Some people, experts and laymen alike, seem to feel that help must have a price tag and that the fair market value can only be stated in millions of dollars. Others feel that social/ emotional help lies only in some professional person's office where three degrees on the wall promise some kind of aid. Too many people today are like Naaman, the Syrian general, who was offended because Elisha's cure for his leprosy was to bathe seven times in the River Jordan. This was not impressive or complex enough to suit Naaman. Yet when he did he was healed. (2 Kings 5: 1-14.)

What healed Naaman? the water of a river? Hardly! He was cured because he obeyed the Lord. President David O. McKay, quoting from the *Life and Teachings of Jesus*, said,

> Spiritual needs can be met only by spiritual means. All governments, laws, methods, and organizations are of no value unless men and women are filled with truth, righteousness, and mercy. Material things have no power to raise the sunken spirit. Gravitation, electricity, and steam are great forces, but they are all powerless to change the motives of men and women.[1]

It is our claim therefore that social and emotional problems based upon behavior not physically or chemically caused can be dealt with successfully by learning and living God's laws.

Many people agree with this statement but only give lip service. For example, they are skeptically tolerant of the bishop or stake president or General Authority who gives instructions such as Elisha gave to Naaman. There are highly educated Latter-day Saint mothers, for example, who are having trouble with their young children, but who never seem to hear the priesthood brethren or the Relief Society president say, "Do not work outside the home, mothers—your children need you!" They continue to work, and their children continue to suffer. Then when the children need extra help they seek a complex cure that often does not include their staying home and being with the children.

---

[1]David O. McKay, *Gospel Ideals* (Salt Lake City: *The Improvement Era*, 1953), p. 391.

This book is built upon some basic premises:

1. That one's spiritual pre-mortal existence and experience has a major bearing on his mortal course of life.

2. That the first eight years of mortal life are given by our Father in heaven as a training period, free of Satan's direct influence, where parents can literally program or educate their children toward adulthood.*

3. That the years from approximately eight to twelve are practice years, under the supervision of parents, but potentially subject to Satan's influence.

4. That from about twelve years on the individual is more and more emotionally independent, so that any retraining or reprogramming can only be done if he is willing. (Prior to this independence, the individual is still quite under the physical and intellectual control of his parents and other adults.)

5. That few social/emotional problems *originate* after the age of twelve.

6. That prior to the age of twelve prevention is possible; however after that stage, therapy or treatment (the cure) is called for when problems reveal themselves, and in most cases the treatment must focus on the present rather than the past.

7. That basic gospel principles and the example set by Father in heaven in dealing with his children can be useful in teaching parents how to take care of their children.

8. That through the structure of the Church, the gospel of Christ, as practiced in healthy Church activity, provides the most effective therapeutic and preventive program available for social/emotional problems.

9. That the individual must choose between the Lord's way and other ways of behavior.

---

*Satan still affects the child's life through environmental influences such as friends, parents, other adults, entertainment, etc. The child, however is not **held** accountable until his eighth year.

These premises are valid only if they are true and agree with the gospel. It is essential to know the gospel, not as some misguided people think it ought to be, but as the scriptures and the Lord's spokesmen reveal it.

One very important key to understanding the Lord's way is to know the difference between eternal, divinely approved ways of living and humanly created ways of living. For the purpose of this discussion the human ways are referred to as "cultural." Culture, in this sense, is developed by men and is usually a mixture of truth and error. For example it is part of man's eternal nature to need love in all its deep and beautiful aspects. It is a cultural factor to try to fill this need only through physical expression. In eternal terms, work is valued because its challenge helps a person grow. It is soul satisfying. In cultural terms work is not valued for it's beneficial effects on the individual, but only as a means for earning a living. Most people see nothing wrong when our society actually denies certain segments of the population—teenagers for example, or some welfare clients—the opportunity to grow through work.

One way to determine the difference between temporary cultural and eternal laws is to compare what *all* human beings do with what only some people do. For example, all people have some form of family life. Not all people who live together are married, though. The family and proper marriage are eternal and instituted by God. Living together without marriage is cultural and instituted by men.

In speaking of sex, an important cultural-versus-eternal difference can be seen. Our Father in heaven instituted the sexual differences between men and women.

> And the rib, which the lord God had taken from man, made he a woman, and brought her unto the man.
> And Adam said, this is now bone of my bones, and flesh of my flesh; she shall be called Woman, because she was taken out of Man.

Therefore shall a man leave his father and his mother, and shall cleave unto his wife: and they shall be one flesh.

And they were both naked, the man and his wife, and were not ashamed. (Gen. 2:22-25.)

He commanded men and women to have children, and he so designed them that they must engage in sexual intercourse to accomplish that goal. When this is done by married people who love each other, it is not only proper but is extremely pleasant and satisfying to both partners. It is clean and wholesome and a treasured gift from the Father. These factors are eternal and of God. In contrast, the present worldly culture permits nudity and open sexual experience to the point of complete degradation. The unclothed human body is now so commonplace that many people no longer respect it. Sexual activity has become open, immodest, and perverted throughout the world.

It is apparent that one style of living is eternal, the other is temporary or cultural. Culture is bad only to the extent that it conflicts with God's eternal laws. The closer the agreement between the two, the higher the level of social/emotional health and well-being in the entire society.

Thus it is suggested that in reading this book and putting principles into practice, great care needs to be given to the source of one's personal ideas. If they are founded on the word of the Lord, they will be effective. If these ideas come from men and do not agree with the Lord's word, one can end up far afield without realizing what happened.

Chapter 2
Basic Personality—Emotional and Mental Factors
Spirits and Computers

Chapter 2

Spirits and Computers

Human development began long before birth. The scriptures and the writings of the prophets—ancient and modern—clearly refer to a premortal state. As spirit children of our Father in heaven we lived with him in the pre-earth heavens and were acquainted with his great wisdom and his completely loving personality.

The scriptures seem to say that one purpose of life prior to mortal birth was education. Perhaps that life could be thought of as elementary school compared to our mortal life, which seems more like college or trade school. In the actual presence of God and his angels, his spirit children prepared to come to the earth.

Some learned more than others, as demonstrated by the ordination of Jesus as the Savior of the world. He had learned enough and progressed far enough to receive this high calling. Others, such as Abraham and Joseph Smith, who were mighty and great, were ordained as prophets.

If these remarkable **beings** were fore-ordained, and if

ordination to any calling is dependent upon worthiness and knowledge, then it logically follows that all of the inhabitants of heaven developed to the point (or failed to develop) where they qualified for a place in mortality or earth life, each at his own appropriate level of knowledge, worthiness, and capacity. Some were fore-ordained bishops. Others acquired the knowledge to be effective leaders of youth, or teachers. "Every man who has a calling to minister to the inhabitants of the world was ordained to that very purpose in the Grand Council of heaven before this world was."[1]

Since all things were created spiritually in heaven before they were created temporally on earth, it follows that the eternal spirits could gain great knowledge before coming to the earth if they so desired. In fact, they may have progressed to the point where they knew—spiritually—everything that man would be permitted to know during this telestial earth life. Thus, prior to mortal birth, each person or spirit had already learned many things in preparation for mortality.

However, to learn a fact in school is quite different from applying that fact to actual life situations. It is like the beginning swimmer. He can practice on dry land for hours, but until he gets his face wet with water trying to flood in through his nose and mouth, until he feels his body sinking without support, he does not really comprehend the meaning of the word *swimming*. As he acquires skill, the word becomes more and more realistic and significant.

So it must have been with education in premortal life. Undoubtedly our spirits were taught about family life, morality, and eternal principles and laws. They had to have enough knowledge to permit them to make a fair choice in the grand council in heaven between the plans of Jesus and Lucifer. (See Pearl of Great Price, Abraham 3:21-28.)

---

[1]Joseph Smith, *Teachings of the Prophet Joseph Smith*, Joseph Fielding Smith, comp. (Salt Lake City: Deseret Book Co., 1965), p. 365.

SPIRITS AND COMPUTERS 13

As they differed in ability and interest, so did their acquisition of knowledge differ. Joseph Smith apparently learned so much so well that he was ready to begin his life's work at fourteen, while most are not ready to start until much later.

One might ask, "What good is premortal education if it is all forgotten at birth?" "But," we must retort, "was that knowledge actually lost?"

Consider the love of Father in heaven and his deep interest in the welfare of his children. Is it consistent with that love for him to send them here stripped of the knowledge they gained through honest, diligent effort? Why do some people have special talents? Where did this brother begin to be so interested in music? Why is that sister such a natural teacher? How can a patriarch tell a twelve-year-old deacon of his strengths long before they develop?

Could it be that one does not forget as much as he may have supposed? Perhaps the veil, which at times seems to be so dense, is really thinner than one dares to imagine.

> Our knowledge of persons and things before we came here, combined with the divinity awakened within our souls through obedience to the gospel, powerfully affects, in my opinion, all our likes and dislikes, and guides our preferences in the course of this life, provided we give careful heed to the admonitions of the Spirit.
>
> All these salient truths which come home so forcibly to the head and heart seem but the awakening of the memories of the spirit. Can we know anything here that we did not know before we came?
>
> ... By the power of the Spirit ... we often catch a spark from the awakened memories of the immortal soul. ... [2]

What a comfort it is to know that all the information necessary to live happily and successfully in this troubled world already lies hidden somewhere within the recesses of the mind. Through study, prayer, and the promptings of the Holy Ghost answers may be found to life's difficult problems.

---

[2] Joseph F. Smith, *Gospel Doctrine* (Salt Lake City: Deseret Book Co., 1968), pp. 12-14.

There is something else to consider. Man has struggled for centuries to define and explore his own mind but still knows very little. Many theories have been advanced in an effort to explain the complex phenomena of human personality. While all of these contain elements of truth, much error creeps in because so few of them accept the concept of a spirit within the body. The word *mind* remains nebulous and ill-defined. Can the scriptures clarify this problem?

The body is literally clay, and upon death or dismemberment becomes, again, dust. Yet when alive, this dust and clay performs wonderous tasks. Why? Part of the body is a marvelously complex control system called the brain, which can either work automatically or can be consciously controlled by the spirit. It can also be controlled to some extent by others, including Satan.

To understand this let us speak briefly of computors. The creation of these mechanical "brains" testifies to God's handiwork. Prior to their manufacture as machines, the elements of computors are just rocks or minerals. Separately these elements hardly resemble the finished computor. Even when assembled, they require trained human operators. Doing this correctly calls for a very important process called programming. This means connecting thousands of wires in a way that permits the machine to "think." In other words, programming is teaching the computor what it needs to know to do its work. Without this, it does nothing useful. If done well, however, the giant collection of elements becomes one of mankind's greatest tools. Without programming it just takes up space and its jobs have to be forgotten or done by many people. Bear in mind also that no matter how grand the machine, it will do nothing until it is given a source of power.

What has this to do with the spirit and body of man? Consider the fact that computors are patterned after the human brain—not mind, but brain. Consider too that the human brain is also clay like the rest of the body, taking up space until it is given a power source. Finally, while power may be available, if the programming or learning is wrong, both machine and brain fail to give true information.

So it is with human beings. To understand man, one needs to understand the relationship of the spirit to the brain, not the "mind" as defined or explained by learned men of the world. One must learn about eternal intelligence and the spirit of man, born of a Father and Mother in heaven.

Joseph Smith stated a great truth when he defined the so-called mind of man more specifically. He said: "I have another subject to dwell upon. . . . It is associated with the subject of the resurrection of the dead—namely . . . the mind of man—the immortal spirit."[3] This spirit has form and substance. It has personality, feelings, and abilities. It is divinely created, eternally existent, and was educated before mortal birth. In the Lord's plan it is temporarily given a shell of clay which it must train or program while living on earth. Man's treatment of his body therefore becomes an important stewardship for which he will some day be called to account.

To help with the programming of his body and brain, the spirit has other characteristics. It knows right from wrong and is endowed with the free agency to choose between them. The immortal spirit also has a conscience and the ability to grow through repentance. This is a basic and important difference between men and animals, or men and machines.

If the spirit trains or programs the brain skillfully, in accordance with divine law, the body becomes so pure that a perfect harmony can exist between them. The spirit and body, being the soul or essence of man, work their way up through the telestial and terrestrial states, and

---

[3]*Teachings of the Prophet Joseph Smith*, p. 352.

eventually can qualify to live with the Father and Jesus Christ in the celestial kingdom.

This is not just a reward for good works. It involves three elements: (1) a knowledge of the laws of God, (2) the will to obey, and (3) the power to control. Harmony of spirit and body is acquired as the laws of God are learned and lived. The higher laws result in a celestial harmony. The lower laws result in a terrestrial or telestial harmony (or perhaps disharmony). As Joseph Smith said, "We consider that God has created man with a mind capable of instruction, and a faculty which may be enlarged in proportion to the heed and diligence given to the light communicated from heaven to the intellect; and that the nearer man approaches perfection, the clearer are his views, and the greater his enjoyments. . . ." (*Teachings,* p. 51.) As the veil between the mature spirit-self and the immature brain becomes thinner, the spirit is able to program more effectively, and the soul becomes a harmonious being, capable of greater and greater work until its mortal purpose is fulfilled and the Father works his will.

What happens then when the spirit and the brain are in conflict? Could this be what is known as a "split personality?" Some professions refer to it as mental illness when Jim Jones seems to be two different people, depending on his mood. The authors prefer to think of it in this discussion as Jim Jones's spirit and brain being out of harmony with each other (and of course with God's laws). This is pure speculation, but many observations tend to bear this out. Disharmony occurs when the information programmed into the brain does not agree with what the spirit learned and vaguely remembers from his premortal life. Also, of course, there are numerous scriptural cases of evil spirits possessing the bodies of men, resulting in bizarre, extreme behavior. Evil spirits cannot control the *spirit* of man unless the person permits it. One prerequisite of mortality was that the spirit could and did overcome Satan in the spirit world. It still has the power to do this. In this life, therefore, Satan attempts to gain control through the body, including the brain. This is another way in which a disharmony may occur, resulting in confusion and possible suffering for the spirit.

What basis is there for this type of thinking? The scriptures clearly state that at mortal birth all are innocent, or clean as a slate is clean before writing upon it. "Every spirit of man was innocent in the beginning; and God having redeemed man from the fall, men became again, in their infant state, innocent before God." (D&C 93:38.) At birth the brain (except for damaged individuals) is a healthy computor waiting to be programmed. The spirit is whole and mature, separated from the brain only by the veil placed there by the Father.

The spirit begins its attempt to program immediately, but for the first eight years of life it requires an immense amount of external help. At birth the human infant is literally helpless and requires assistance even to breathe and eat. Initially, this is his greatest struggle, but as his brain is programmed by each passing day's experiences, he is capable of doing more for himself. Eventually he walks, talks, and provides for himself—if all goes well in programming. If there is trouble—improper programming—then he is handicapped. His brain is sending out confusing information.

For example, if a tiny infant does not receive enough cuddling and other programming showing affection, its brain somehow sends out signals that cause the infant to begin to waste away and possible eventually to die. This is called 'marasmus' and is very real, especially in large orphanages in earlier years.

During World War II, war orphans were sometimes placed in institutions until homes could be found for them. In one of these in England a whole room full of young babies were found to be fretful, losing weight, and generally unhealthy except for one child who was normal, happy and responsive. Upon investigation this child was found to be the favorite of one of the nurses who picked him up often, held him close, and talked to him lovingly. After the doctor ordered this kind of treatment for all the babies, the others began to gain weight, cry less, and improve in general health and development.

At every stage of human mortal development there are basic needs which, if not met properly, result in programming which is crippling to the personality and which affects the individual's entire life. It is possible to reprogram the brain, or at least to modify the original programming, but the older the person the more difficult this becomes. Many professions have developed, such as social work, psychology, and psychiatry, to help people reprogram. In fact some encouraging results are being seen through technical methods known as reality therapy, operant conditioning, and other similar methods. The authors have no quarrel with these encouraging trends, as long as the salvation of the individual is the paramount concern of the therapist. This means that any behavior modifications which occur must not interfere with free agency or human dignity. However, the Lord prefers that the job of programming be done properly in the first place, at home, by mother and father.

Every mother who voluntarily elects to give her child to others to raise while she works implies that she will permit much of her child's programming to be done without her direct supervision. What guarantee does she have that he will be taught correct principles? This unique programming of the mortal brain occurs only once in all eternity, yet many mothers (and fathers) freely choose to let someone else do it for them.

To sum up then, if men learn principles in childhood which are in harmony with God's laws—those learned by the spirit in premortal life—their adult years are usually productive and happy. If incorrect principles are learned the individual becomes enmeshed, in varying degrees, in the social and emotional ills so evident on every hand. Everyone experiences this to some extent. Some people can reprogram and pretty well overcome their difficulties by themselves. Others need a great deal of help.

This means that if Brother Jones is so mentally ill (without a physical or chemical cause) that he seems to be two different people, then he is probably the victim of a struggle between his divine, mature spirit and his mortal, immature computor or brain.

It means that if Sister Smith does not seem to show love to her husband and children, (even though she probably learned of love in the pre-existence, because God *is* love) her early mortal programming may have occurred in a home where love did not abide. This means that her struggling spirit, which was taught about love in heaven and which knows that love is the great law upon which all other laws hang, is dealing with a brain that has not learned about love. Thus, Sister Smith learns to react with fear, suspicion, and hurt because that is how her unloving home environment programmed her in childhood years.

At this point, the reader may well ask what can be done if someone is improperly programming his children or if someone has already been improperly programmed.

One hope of this book is to identify those effective ways in which the programs of the Church and the gospel in general can help, through correct programming or reprogramming, to achieve that harmony of spirit and body which leads to eternal life and joy.

Please bear in mind that while our ultimate goal is celestial joy the journey here below is far more satisfying and happy if lived according to God's laws. It is not necessary to wait for the resurrection to experience a semblance of heaven (or hell for that matter).

Chapter 3
Love, the Great Commandment

Chapter 3

Love: the Great Commandment

Ann Jones sat on the edge of her chair anxiously wringing her hands. Her attractive face was pale and taut, her body shaken every few minutes by deep sobbing. Finally, after many attempts, she cried, "My parents never have loved me!" With this she held her shaking head in her hands and broke down. Was this a child or teenager? No, Ann was a thirty-year-old college graduate who was facing the possible breakup of her temple marriage. She had many serious personal problems and had come for professional help as suggested by her bishop.

When the counselor had completed the evaluation of Ann's problems, his conclusion was precisely what she had dramatically said it was. Her parents never loved her. More precisely, she did not *feel* loved by her parents.

Why does it matter so much to an adult, especially a so-called educated and sophisticated "modern" woman, whether her parents loved her or not? Why do her doubts permit so much unhappiness to enter her life? What part does love play in other human problems, especially today when the word means so many things to different people?

What is love? The answer is deceptively simple. John the Beloved said, "God is love" (1 John 4:8), implying that God personifies the concept and the application of love. The scriptures say that spirit, light, and truth shine forth from God to give light and life to all things. (See D&C 88:6, 7, 11, 13.) Is love also a basic attribute of this light and life giving spirit? ". . . If we love one another, God dwelleth in us, and his love is perfected in us. Hereby know we that we dwell in him, and he in us, because he hath given us of his spirit." (1 John 4:12-13.)

The Savior and God the Father are two separate and distinct beings, yet the Savior said, ". . . thou, Father, art in me, and I in thee. . . ." (John 17:21.) This seems to indicate an intermingling of the spirit, which is not contained within the physical body, but which emanates out and is life-giving and sustaining.

Human beings also have spirits that shine forth in proportion to their capacity to love. Some people glow, some people flicker like a candle, some are in spiritual darkness.

When two people love one another, this too is a reaching out, an intermingling of the spirit. This, too, is exhilarating and life giving. It is a form of nourishment to the soul. To break up a romance or to lose a loved one is a form of spiritual deprivation. The spirit goes hungry until other sources of emotional support can be found. People can become mentally ill from lack of love. Babies can die. The spirit literally withers away from starvation.

An example of this was reported regarding American prisoners of war in North Korea. They were systematically denied any form of hope or encouragement. In letters from home everything was deleted except bad news. They were forced to endure regular sessions of self-criticism, dwelling on their faults and shortcomings. Those who showed natural leadership were separated from the others.

Their captors then tried to supply the missing friendship and love so they would think communism was desirable. A few accepted this and defected. Some were able to resist but became mentally ill. Some lay down and died, from no physiological causes.

In today's frantic, confused world what practical good is it to say, "God is love"? Does this really help? A leading news magazine, recently discussing the serious human problems in large cities, made the statement that money was the only solution—higher wages, more federal grants, more money. Nowhere was love even mentioned, though the problems discussed involved people and their treatment of each other.

In the scriptures we read:

Then one of them, which was a lawyer, asked him a question, tempting him and saying,
Master, which is the great commandment in the law?
Jesus said unto him, Thou shalt love the Lord thy God with all thy heart, and with all thy soul, and with all thy mind.
This is the first and great commandment.
And the second is like unto it, Thou shalt love thy neighbor as thyself.
On these two commandments hand all the law and the prophets. (Matt. 22:35-40.)

The Savior himself said, "On these two commandments hang *all* the law and the prophets." Not part, not some, but all!

Taking this statement for what it truly means, can it be applied to human problems? All other laws rest upon the law of *love*; those laws are then not valid without love. This is a strong statement to make, but consider the writings of Paul:

And though I have the gift of prophecy, and understand all mysteries, and all knowledge; and though I have all faith, so that I could remove mountains, and have not charity [love] I am nothing. (1 Cor. 13:2.)

These scriptures must be taken seriously, and not in any way rationalized. **They mean what they say!**

Referring back to Naaman and his seven baths—many people today want great, impressive projects to solve the problems facing mankind, when the real need is probably seven trips to the Jordan. Men need to obey the laws of God. They need to love each other. It is so simple, yet the world has not been able to do this on any large scale. As one man said, "Christianity isn't a failure; it just hasn't been tried yet."

Since love is the greatest commandment and the basis for successful mortality, it must, as with the prisoners and babies referred to previously, logically follow that its absence causes unhappiness in a person's life. Its presence, on the other hand, leads to a sense of well-being based upon good mental health. If a large proportion of the people are happy because they are mentally healthy, the society itself will reflect this. Social problems will be at a minimum.

What does it mean then to love one's fellowmen? Until love is demonstrated in concrete ways and recognized as love by the other person, the words remain meaningless. There are two parts to love, and both are necessary. It is not enough just to feel inside one's heart. One must also *give of himself.* To a loving spirit, the feeling and the doing are inseparably connected. Being kind, generous, and helpful is as natural as breathing. When an unloving person goes through the motions without feeling love in his heart, the acts may be appreciated, but the other person will not feel loved. Insincerity always shines through and destroys the effectiveness of the act. *The experience of love is one key to human mental health.* It blesses him who gives and him who receives.

A person learns to love by having been loved. As the warmth of affection reaches through to the hungry spirit, feelings of confidence and self-worth grow. With the assurance that all is well within himself, the individual can turn his thoughts outward. He can feel truly loving toward other people.

Ideally, a person learns how to love in his own home, with his own family. Unfortunately, this does not always happen. Some people grow to adulthood feeling fearful *even if* and unacceptable to others. Their thoughts and feelings *their mothers* turn back in upon themselves in morbid preoccupation. *were home* They are unable to give love to others.

All people, however, are loved by their Father in heaven. If they really believed this, what a difference it would make in their lives!

> Herein is love, not that we loved God, but that he loved us, and sent his son to be the propitiation of our sins.
>
> Beloved, if God so loved us, we ought also to love one another.
>
> And we have known and believed the love that God has to us. God is love; and he that dwelleth in love, dwelleth in God, and God in him. (1 John 4:10-11, 16.)

Love is closely related to the previous discussion about the spirit, the computor, and man's brain. To better understand this, think of all emotions as providing different degrees of well-being. Toward one end of the scale lie those emotions considered healthy (love, confidence, compassion). At the other end are unhealthy emotions (fear, hatred, anger). In between are many degrees, going all the way from healthy to sick.

As a person goes from the healthy end of the scale toward the sick end of the scale, he literally loses love. The important people in his life, such as mother, father, wife, do not successfully convey love to him. He does not know what love is because he does not experience it. Into his brain is programmed a feeling of personal unworthiness and a forlorn loneliness. He cannot believe that other people love him. He neither gives love nor receives it.

Another way to express this is that love is a manifestation of the spirit of Christ that dwells within. Conversely, when one permits fear, hatred, anger, frustration, depression and other negative emotions to remain with him, this is an invitation to the adversary to enter, to intensify the emotions and confuse the issues so that the individual cannot understand why he feels as he does. When the divine spirit gains control, it can cast out the bad feelings before Satan has a chance to take over. If Satan does slip in unnoticed, a strong spirit can cast him out too. President David O. McKay spoke often of self-control. ". . . Jealousy, hatred, envy, animosity—all such evils you must overcome by suppression. That is where your control comes in. Suppress that anger! Suppress that jealousy, that envy! They are all injurious to the spirit anyhow." (*Gospel Ideals*, p. 356.)

In this sense positive and negative emotions represent a power struggle for control of the body. Man can align himself with the loving spirit of God or he can use his free agency in the other direction. Most people think emotions just happen and that nothing can be done about them. This is far from the truth. The human spirit has, or can develop, power and strength to make of his life what he wills. This is, however, a lifelong struggle. To sit back and just let things happen means losing the battle by default. The whole picture is further confused by the strong appetites and passions of the body itself. For the spirit to learn to control in the direction of God and love is essential to human happiness and mental health.

For example, the mentally ill person usually knows he has problems. He is so aware of them that he is literally terrified. In fact, much of his surface behavior is due to his fear and anxiety. Does love terrify? Of course it doesn't. Love warms the soul and expands the heart. It gives hope and courage. "There is no fear in love; but perfect love casteth out fear; because fear hath torment. He that feareth is not made perfect in love." (1 John 4:18.)

Thus, when a warm, helpful person reaches out to a disturbed person, healing begins. This can be a janitor or a psychiatrist, depending on his ability to give love.

Without love, men fear, hate, quarrel, and put a price tag on everything they do. With love, men serve, help, and give to each other without reservation. The Savior's love has no price tag, it is unconditional. It is not based upon material success or even upon righteous endeavors. He loves his children whatever they are. Nevertheless, when they live his commandments they *earn* a closer relationship with him.

Feeling and experiencing love is a protection and insulation from life's worst blows. Its presence is a powerful weapon in life's battle. Its absence is painful and destructive.

Love is not expressed the same way by all people, nor is it received in the same way. Its manifestation varies as widely as the human family.

As Linus in the comic strip "Peanuts" says: "Happiness is an old blanket." Love, or the development of it, can be this basic.

To an infant, love is a dry diaper, a warm bottle, a gentle voice and soft arms.

To the one-year-old love is a favorite toy. It is being allowed to splatter food all over his face as he learns to feed himself.

The five-year-old sees love in dad's rough horseplay, or a Sunday School teacher's praise for a halting prayer.

At eight years, love is dad's baptizing and confirming Mary or playing ball with Johnny; it is mother's punishing Johnny for wrong-doing and hugging him after he gets the point.

At twelve, love can be mother's understanding ear as Mary tries to explain why her feelings were hurt at school, or dad's firm but loving patience when John falls down in his school grades.

At eighteen, love is an intimate but respectful association between a young man and young woman.

In marriage love is a husband and wife growing together. It is opening the car door, feeding the baby at 2:00 a.m., and tenderly sharing each other sexually.

Ideally, love will increase and grow stronger day by day. It is not a theory or a sermon. It is doing! It is the expression of the divine spirit through noble acts. Love as a mere feeling is like a seed. It flowers and becomes a living reality when it is acted upon in life. It is inconsistent, for example, to be proud of Church activity if that activity does not include helping other people in real and concrete ways.

We live in an age when this beautiful concept of love has been hideously disfigured. One of the most common phrases today is "making love," referring to sexual intercourse. Marriage manuals by so-called experts have titles promising "marriage advice," when the contents actually deal only with the mechanical aspects of sexual relations. Many, many people equate marriage with the sex act. In truth, this is only one part of the much greater whole of marriage and family life. What the world so often considers "making love" is in reality just a physical experience.

Sexual relations are extremely important if the purpose is to show love not only toward the partner but also toward those spirits who may gain mortal bodies because of the sexual union of man and woman. In the Lord's eternal wisdom the act of sex is an emotional and passionate experience; but without the spiritual understanding which is true love, it is only a physical thing and actually quite unrewarding for either party.

Another deeply unfortunate perversion of love by our modern culture (indeed by cultures through the ages) is intimate physical activity between persons of the same sex, or homosexuality. It is the Lord's command that men love men and women love women because we are brothers and sisters. But He has never even suggested that this love be perverted to include sexual acts. Homosexuality in adults is a sickness and should be treated that way. Those who try to claim that it is a legitimate form of sexual expression are themselves either sick or tools of Satan. Paul warned against this long ago.

> Be not deceived: neither fornicators, nor idolators, nor adulterers, nor effeminate, nor abusers of themselves with mankind.

LOVE: THE GREAT COMMANDMENT

Nor thieves, nor covetous, nor drunkards, nor revilers, nor extortioners, shall inherit the kingdom of God. (1 Cor. 6:9-10.)

Paul puts these unholy sexual acts in with some rough company, and that is where they should be. Nevertheless, though the sin is hated, the sinner must be loved and helped to reach a mental condition permitting healthy sexual behavior.

Still another serious perversion of so-called love involves incest, or sexual activity between close blood relatives, especially parent and child. This is a terrible sin and a grave emotional blow to a child. Whenever such an act has occurred, the child feels extremely guilty and unworthy, and has serious difficulty in later years, especially with self-respect. Great care and love are needed to understand all the factors and to help a child so afflicted.

[margin note: who defines the relationship? 1st cousins?]

As can be seen, the world at large has drifted a long way from the idea of love as the manifestation of the life-giving spirit of Christ intermingling with the spirits of men and blossoming forth in charitable acts.

"And the love of men shall wax cold, and iniquity shall abound." (D&C 45:27.) It does not need to be so. It must not remain so.

*[margin notes:
simplistic general assertions (untested)

Love ≠ sex
Love ↔ exploitation?
Love = giving? (for what purpose?) (of what?)]*

Chapter 4
The First Year of Life
Infancy: Introduction to Mortality

Chapter 4

Infancy: Introduction to Mortality

The first year of a child's life is most vital in laying the foundation for future mental health. To develop a general attitude of trust toward himself and others is his first task. Newborn Johnny and all other healthy infants begin, hopefully, to develop confidence in the world as a pleasant place in which to live.

Erik Erikson, a psychologist of note, has further explained how trusting others leads to trust of oneself. Speaking of a young child, he says:

> In his gradually increasing waking hours he finds that more and more adventures of the senses arouse a feeling of familiarity, of having coincided with an inner goodness. Forms of comfort, and people associated with them, become . . . familiar. . . . Such consistency, continuity, and sameness of experience provide a rudimentary sense of ego identity. . . .[1]

In the framework of the gospel this principle is called *faith*. It is a basic principle. Without this, the children of men would be lost in a world they could not understand. So it is that young children need faith in the adults

---

[1] Erik H. Erickson, *Child and Society* (New York: Norton & Co., 1963), p. 247.

around them. This enables them to accept with confidence what they do not understand. Faith in oneself lays the groundwork for the full use of one's capabilities but faith in parents is basic to warm relationships with other people and later to faith in God and must precede faith in oneself.

In the scriptures we find the following:

> I waited patiently for the Lord; and he inclined unto me and heard my cry.
> Blessed is that man that maketh the Lord his trust. . . . (Psalm 40:1, 4.)
> . . . Then shall thy confidence wax strong in the presence of God. . . . (D&C 121:45.)

As the Lord inspires confidence in his children, so ought parents to be worthy of the trust and confidence of their offspring! This begins at birth.

Our subject Johnny receives quite a shock passing from his mother's womb. He emerges into very different surroundings. The feelings he develops as this new environment strikes him begin immediately to program his brain. Johnny's computor is now being fed all manner of data. As it prints upon his brain, his mortal self begins its very rapid development.

At first everything is probably a blur of sights and sounds. Gradually his eyes focus, and he discovers objects. Soon he learns to reach out, to touch, then to grasp. This enables him to associate ideas. His blanket is soft. His bottle is hard. The sides of his crib are smooth. Sounds also begin to make sense. His mother's voice, now associated with warmth, comfort, and love, brings forth his first real smile. Others smile in return. He can communicate! He is no longer a stranger in a strange land. His loving spirit receives the precious nourishment it needs to grow.

Johnny has other needs, however. Initially, these are quite basic. He requires food, oxygen, and a comfortable bed for sleep. He also needs warmth and dryness, especially while he is in diapers. Gentle physical contact with other human beings, the tenderness of his mother's arms, the strength of his father, bring secure feelings and an awareness of being loved.

As his muscles grow he discovers that his body is a valuable tool. He can do some things for himself! He doesn't have to wait for someone to bring him a toy! From the moment of birth his goal is to grow up and become an independent, capable human being. He is obeying the principle of eternal progression.

At this stage his play is his work. What appears to be random, meaningless actions, or even naughtiness, is often a form of experimenting, trying out, practicing. Why does he tire so quickly of an expensive new toy? After he finds out how it feels, tastes, sounds, and smells, is familiar with how it looks from every angle, what else is there to learn? His inquiring mind wants new challenges, and a spoon out of the kitchen drawer may be just as interesting as a ten dollar toy—maybe more so.

Why does Johnny keep throwing all his toys out of his crib? Maybe he has just rediscovered the law of gravity. It is very fascinating to find out that some things fall faster than others, and that a block makes a nice loud bang when it hits the floor, whereas a blanket makes no sound at all!

An understanding of why children do what they do is essential if parents expect to help with the proper programming of Johnny's computer-brain. To be punished for trying to learn causes frustration and rage. It encourages mental laziness and helplessness. Doing everything for the child instead of letting him learn to do for himself produces the same results. If continued, the idea is eventually programmed into his brain that "I am incompetent and useless. I can't do anything." Thus are sown the seeds for the lack of self-respect experienced later by many people with social and emotional problems.

How else does faulty programming take place? Although his needs at first appear to be mostly physical, a very subtle process is occurring emotionally. For example, if Johnny's diapers get wet and cold and remain that way, his brain may be programmed to think of the environment as cold and unpleasant. If his diapers are changed, then his brain gradually learns that life seems to involve occasional discomfort followed by eventual relief. There are rough spots along with the smooth.

Johnny's development is healthy if his little computor is programmed to expect mostly good times, but imagine how difficult his life will be if his brain knows only bad times. The spirit, struggling to relate these feelings to the half-remembered loving experiences which he knew with his Father in heaven before he came here, becomes frustrated and confused. He knows that something is terribly wrong.

Every child is sensitive to the emotional atmosphere in his home. Johnny cries during the night. Loud angry voices approach. He feels pain as he is slapped! For Johnny the world is becoming an unpleasant place. He is learning fear instead of trust.

To be able to tolerate a child's crying when it interferes with one's own needs or comfort requires patience and understanding. Immature parents confuse children by alternating between lavish spoiling when they are in a good mood and harsh rejection or neglect when their needs are in opposition to those of the child.

For example, Johnny's mother may have had a big argument with her neighbor and come into the house angry and upset, only to find Johnny demanding attention by crying loudly. This further irritation may cause her to take out her pent-up anger on Johnny, who is small and helpless and cannot fight back. What she needs right now is some sympathy, not a crying baby! If she frequently gives way to her own feelings and does become angry and harsh, acting kind and loving only when this

good

happens to suit her mood, imagine the conflict in Johnny's brain! What eventually gets programmed is that people are inconsistent, unreliable, unfair, and perhaps even cruel. Besides breeding insecurity, this will be a real handicap when Johnny gets old enough to be aware of other people. He will expect them to be like his parents, and skillful reprogramming will be required to convince him otherwise!

One little girl was saved from the consequences of the violation of fundamental principles by her wise, inspired bishop.

Ruth J., one year old, was extremely nervous, cried constantly, and did not eat well. Ruth was born into a family with many problems. Her parents were both very insecure people who had received little or no love in their own childhoods. In fact they were so unhappy and confused that their behavior bordered on that area called schizophrenic. While trying to appear normal, in their own desperate way they were deteriorating toward mental illness and divorce, and were infecting Ruth in the process. With four children, they were confused by parenthood and unable to cope with the demands of housekeeping, regular employment, church activity, and the general pressures of living. Brother J. was an elders quorum president, a returned missionary, and a college graduate. Sister J. held a Sunday School position and was also a college graduate. They had been married in the temple. While putting up a good front, they fought constantly at home. Their inability to handle ordinary life situations was demoralizing. Finally, Brother J. threw a table lamp at his wife. Fortunately, it missed her, but it broke the front room window. She ran around the corner to the bishop's home for refuge, after which the bishop became actively involved.

This family's wounds were deep and required extensive help, but Ruth's problems demanded immediate attention. She was thin, jumpy, emotionless, and obviously suffering from lack of warm, affectionate attention. Her mother seldom held her, and never in a cuddling way. It was unlikely that Ruth had ever heard lullabies or been allowed to sleep in her mother's arms. Her feedings were mechanical and brief.

Such treatment, unless counteracted, would certainly cause Ruth to be severely disturbed in later years. She would have difficulty trusting and loving anyone. Her spirit's deep unmet need for the nourishment of loving relationships might easily push her into shallow sexual escapades. Even if she were fortunate enough to remain active in the Church and marry in the temple, she might deprive her husband and children of healthy love and be unable to cope with the problems this would create. Not being able to give or receive true love, she would probably pass her sickness on to her children.

Helping Brother and Sister J. through the Church program took many forms. Because of the severity of their emotional problems, the bishop first referred them to a Church-oriented professional, who interviewed them intensively on three occasions. These interviews brought the basic issues out in the open, where the J's admitted their fears, lack of self-esteem, and great need for love. With this evaluation the bishop then assigned a stable and patient home teacher who became a true friend to Brother J. He also asked the Relief Society president to assign warm Relief Society visiting teachers, who were able to teach Sister J. how to give Ruth the love and attention she critically needed.

The bishop helped them recognize and discuss the irritations in their lives and set goals; for example, Brother J. was contemptuous of his wife's housekeeping, although he failed to maintain the yard and car. The bishop kindly, but firmly, suggested that Brother J. devote attention to his yard work and that, day by day, he practice not commenting on Sister J.'s housekeeping. The first full day free of criticism so relieved Sister J. that she began to do better house work for the "fun" of it.

The bishop gave Brother J. welfare assignments from the ward executive committee which helped him to develop concern for those people he helped; for example, an elderly widow's home needed repainting. The widow benefited from the company of the quorum members, especially Brother J.

Sister J. was released from the Sunday School and given special Relief Society assignments that challenged her but were still within her capacity. As she succeeded, she developed self-respect, which made her less vulnerable to her husband's criticism and at the same time more interesting to him. His critical comments decreased. Gradually they began to fill the vacuum in their lives as true love and understanding grew between them.

Finally, once each month the bishop orally evaluated the J's very briefly, but frankly, not permitting them to ignore pressure points.

The results of all this work over many months were twofold: one effect was, of course, a happier family; the other was that Ruth began to relax, play, smile, and eat because her happier mother was holding and cuddling her. Ruth was finally being treated like a baby instead of an object.

It is interesting to note that Ruth's treatment never did involve direct work with her by the bishop or his associates. This demonstrates the importance of parental influences. Happy parents tend to have happy, healthy children.

Part of this important influence depends upon the basic attitudes of the parents toward their children. Some consider children a sacred right and privilege and find them very rewarding. Others gain their major life satisfactions outside the home away from children. For this parent, the needs and wants of children and sometimes of the spouse are sacrificed for success in the husband's career or the wife's Church activities. It is the feeling that "everything in the world is more important than I am" that programs the idea of futility and worthlessness into Johnny's brain. Some youngsters feel like second class citizens in their own homes.

Also, when Johnny is left with a succession of baby sitters, each one will handle him differently. When one permits him to do what another scolds him for doing, confusion and insecurity are programmed. Later on Johnny will learn that some people are friendly and some are not, and that all people are different. The first year of his life, however, is not the best time to learn this Trust and security must come first.

Of course it is possible for parents who are quite busy to avoid this pitfall by taking good advantage of the time they do spend at home. Each parent should take a few minutes every day to talk to individual children, to listen, to teach, and to learn from them. Brigham Young, even while carrying the heavy responsibilities of prophet and president, was never too busy to listen to his children. Such consistent reassurance will convince Johnny that he really is important and well-loved.

Should this be of concern to Latter-day Saint parents? The Lord said that his work and glory was to bring to pass the immortality and eternal life of his children. (See Moses 1:39.) When a young couple marry in the temple, they start their celestial family. What is *their* work and glory?

Think about this. Most men experience great satisfaction from gaining success in their chosen professions. It brings honor, prestige, worldly comforts, the satisfaction of achieving and developing talents. All of these goals are much sought after in today's world. If, however, a man had to choose between these and the eternal welfare of his family, which would come first? In the world at large family closeness and strength is being sacrificed every day. Children are growing up unloved, insecure, lonely, rebellious.

"After all, to do well those things which God ordained

to be the common lot of all man-kind, is the truest greatness. To be a successful father or a successful mother is greater than to be a successful general or a successful statesman." (*Gospel Doctrine*, p. 285.)

High achievement is exceedingly worthwhile, but not at the expense of one's family.

What about young mothers? If they work outside the home or become excessively involved in church work, the situation may be the same. Many women in today's world have difficulty in accepting their roles of wife and mother. The world tells them that their basic concern should be for themselves. Is it important for a woman to feel fulfilled as a person? Of course it is. The tragedy is that many wives and mothers cannot see beyond the routine drudgery of house work to the supreme joys of assisting Father in heaven with his plans for his children.

Even if a woman does not feel personally fulfilled through motherhood, she should realize that the magnitude of the task is something for which it is a privilege to make a personal sacrifice. Think of all the social problems that can be *prevented* through the proper care and training of children. The world culture is so oriented to selfish pleasure that one needs to remember the importance of personal responsibility. Keeping in mind ultimate goals helps a mother cope with small irritations. There are tasks that must be done even though they are not enjoyable at the moment. The satisfaction of a job well done, or the pain of seeing one's children in trouble will come later.

Sometimes Latter-day Saint mothers go to the other extreme and are so concerned and protective that they do not help their children to grow up into competent, self-reliant adults. When these young people graduate from high school and leave home for work, college, or military service, they are quite unprepared for the problems they will face.

"Motherhood lies at the foundation of happiness in

the home, and of prosperity in the nation. God has laid upon men and women very sacred obligations with respect to motherhood, and they are obligations that cannot be disregarded without involking divine displeasure." (*Gospel Doctrine,* p. 288.)

A further attitude to consider is how a parent views parenthood. If a mother knows that her crying, struggling little ball of energy is a gift from God, her conduct toward that infant will be on a far higher plane than if she is aware only of his tears, his demands, and her tired back. Parents need to remember that children are their brothers and sisters from the spirit world. Since they are only temporarily physically immature, they are deserving of respect and help. Later in adulthood, these children become friends, counselors, and mature associates in highly satisfying ways.

Some parents think of a child as a toy, to be played with at will and possibly neglected at other times. For others he is a lump of clay, to form and mold into some preconceived idea of what he must become. Still other parents see him as an extension of themselves, belonging to them and existing for the purpose of filling the emotional needs of the parents.

The first of these types program insecurity and mistrust into their children. The second and third cannot let the child be himself and fulfill his own unique potential. This is not the plan of our Father in heaven. One's own personality is a sacred right of every human being.

> . . . And one man shall not build upon another's foundation, neither journey in another's track. (D&C 52:33.)
>
> Independent action is essential to every man's success or failure.
>
> It is easy to see what a sad condition the world would be in if Lucifer's plan had succeeded. . . . Every soul would have become a nonentity; individuality would have been destroyed. . . .
>
> Compulsion is a thing foreign to the kingdom of God.[2]

---

[2] Joseph Fielding Smith, *The Way to Perfection* (Salt Lake City: The Genealogical Society of Utah, 1935), pp. 179-80.

We should not conclude, however, that children can be permitted to have their own way all the time and that parents must not influence their children for good. There must be limits and supervision, it is true. The subject of discipline, however, does not apply too much to the first year of a child's life. Whatever mistakes he makes are from a lack of knowledge. *Teach* him. Tell him patiently. Show him!

During the first year, observance of free agency means letting Johnny play with what interests him most, encouraging exploration, and letting him grow at his own rate and in his own way. His fierce determination to learn for himself can be a real asset. Always there must be limits, however. He may not destroy property; he may not hurt other children; he must be protected from danger. He cannot be allowed to abuse others with his temper.

To add one note about general development: at this stage, and at all other stages of growth, a physical inventory should be taken. The family doctor should see Johnny regularly to detect and deal with physical problems. This should not be overlooked! Remember that a strong, healthy body is necessary for optimum functioning of the spirit.

> The Church teaches that everyone should regard his body as 'the temple of God'; and that he maintain it's purity and sanctity as such. He is taught that the spirit of the Lord dwells not in unclean tabernacles; and that therefore he is required to live according to the laws of health which constitute part of the law of God.[3]

Although the needs of young children are crucial, no parents should be expected to neglect their own health or to completely ignore their own interests. A balance needs to be achieved. To be left with a competent baby sitter once in awhile not only does not hurt Johnny, but may add to his security. It teaches him that there are other

---
[3]James E. Talmage, *The Articles of Faith* (Salt Lake City: The Church of Jesus Christ of Latter-day Saints, 1924), p. 447.

good people in the world with whom he can feel safe and secure. If mother is there most of the time, the basic programming will not be confused.

The stress and strain of first-year parenthood makes a change of pace for father, and especially for mother, essential. Johnny suffers if he thinks he is the only important person in the family and that all life revolves around his every need. Mother's attendance at Relief Society pays a bonus for Johnny, as does Dad's priesthood work.

It is no virtue for a woman to say she is always home. She can be there 24 hours a day and feel so miserable that she is a negative influence in Johnny's life. Since her attitude while at home is so important, both she and Johnny's father should be aware of her need for some variety and recreation. She needs to plan for some time to herself to do what she likes to do best. She and her husband need time alone together to talk and to keep alive their loving relationship.

This early developmental period lasts roughly throughout the first year of life and is basic to further healthy growth. Although Johnny is soaking up knowledge at an astounding rate, without proper initial programming of the brain he will be in trouble. In this period of development, as in any other, if disharmony occurs between the spirit and the brain, development from then on is potentially more difficult. Human beings are very strong emotionally, however, and single, isolated incidents seldom ruin a life. It is the accumulation of destructive incidents that eventually result in mental illness or emotional instability. Fortunately for parents and for youth leaders, children are flexible and can survive quite a bit of faulty programming without serious handicapping.

Parents are not alone in their child raising efforts. The Church of Jesus Christ of Latter-day Saints is uniquely structured so as to give assistance to families. Even before Johnny is born, the Church can help prepare his mortal home. Through the traditional growth-producing steps of the gospel fostered by the MIA and Sunday School, or through special teaching by home teachers, Relief Society workers, and bishops, Johnny's expectant parents can learn thrilling facts about children and parenthood. "But little children are holy, being sanctified through the atonement of Jesus Christ; and this is what the scriptures mean." (D&C 74:7.) "Suffer little children, and forbid them not, to come unto me: for of such is the kingdom of heaven." (Matthew 19:14.)

Johnny's first birthday is usually a great event. He has progressed from an inert little bundle that mostly sleeps, crys, and eats, to a real personality who is making his presence felt more and more. His second year is an equally important transition year in which he grows out of babyhood and into a mischievous little boy. What new challenges lie ahead?

Chapter 5

Early Childhood
Two Through Four

Trial and Error

Chapter 5

Trial and Error

Johnny is now entering his second year. The stage of development into which he is emerging will last approximately until his fourth year. This is a *doing* stage.

As he grows and gains further control over his body, he discovers that he can do more and more things for himself. He can walk, he can climb, he can feed himself quite well. His world is expanding rapidly. His surroundings offer endless opportunities for exploration and discovery. There are many skills to learn.

Language gives him a sense of power as he shouts "no" and adults pay attention. Already Johnny is learning to manipulate grownups through endless dawdling, refusal to eat, throwing temper tantrums, and asking for drinks of water or other services after he has been put to bed.

This is a conflicting stage in which he is torn between wanting the complete attention given to him when he was a small baby and feeling the need to be more independent and to do for himself. He does not know that at each stage of development one must give up something of the past in order to move into the new maturities of the future.

What has happened is that Johnny has become aware of himself as a separate person. His overriding need is to find his place in the family. "How do I fit into this family? How important am I compared to everyone else?" he might ask. A sense of order and security develops when he discovers that there are definite and consistent rules about what he may or may not do.

Johnny pushes to the limit to find answers to these questions. If there are no firm limits against which to push, he becomes confused. Programmed into his brain are the ideas, "I may do anything I choose to do" and "The whole world revolves around me." Obviously, these attitudes will lead to endless conflicts with other people.

If, on the other hand, the parents constantly yell at him and call him a naughty boy, into his brain will go the information that everything he does is wrong and that he is so bad that no one likes him. This negative opinion of himself and his abilities will be particularly damaging to future development.

Although child psychologists and child development specialists have different names and different descriptions of this period, all agree that it is a crucial stage. Skillful handling when discipline first becomes an issue can save parents untold grief in future years.

To turn now to the framework of the gospel of Jesus Christ, how can Johnny's behavior at this stage be explained? Are there any clues as to how he should be handled? Certain gospel principles apply at all stages of growth and are used by Father in heaven in dealing with his children. Some of these are eternal progression, obedience, free agency, unity, and prayer (communication). Faith was introduced in chapter 4. Repentance is not pertinent until after age eight.

Starting first with eternal progression as applied to a

two-year-old, parents should never forget that underneath much of Johnny's behavior is the urge to grow.

James L. Hymes in his book *Understanding Your Child* describes this in a most delightful way.

> Look at them when they are born, and they can't budge from where you put them. Look at them six years later and they won't stay in one place!
>
> Nobody teaches them. Nobody makes them. Nobody rewards or punishes them. Nobody persuades. It happens!
>
> ... More important: they *want* to grow.
>
> Eating? "Me do it" I can pour my own milk. . . .
>
> Dressing? "Me do it" I can button my own buttons. . . .
>
> There is even more. *Children want to learn.* The fire inside them includes that too. . . .
>
> You live with them and you have to be a walking Solomon. . . .
>
> He uses his tongue. He uses his eyes. He uses his hands. . . .
>
> It is the adult who keeps saying, "No," and the child who persists. . . .
>
> An urge to grow. An urge to know. And an equal urge to be skilled. . . .
>
> But children are practicers, earnest ones and diligent. It is inside of them. Mastery is the thing that matters. They are made so that they desperately need to get good at things. . . .
>
> Of course this does not mean—it could not mean—that what children want to get skilled at will be identical with what adults want them to learn. . . .
>
> Many, many times we miss the boat. We are ahead of children, behind them, or alongside. What looks important to us is so much noise to them. And what they are willing to give time to is unimportant to us.[1]

Much of Johnny's "naughty" behavior is just his urge to practice, to grow, to learn, coming in conflict with what parents think he should be learning or doing.

Parents need to keep in mind that if they want to help Johnny grow, the word *no* should be used sparingly, but used firmly when it is used. Cooperation is a two-way street.

Parents co-operate with children when they help the children find the right time and place to do what they like, *without* causing

---

[1]James L. Hymes, *Understanding Your Child* (Englewood Cliffs, N.J.: Prentice Hall, 1952), pp. 4-10, 12, 13.

inconvenience, discomfort or damage. Most of what children would like to do is not wrong in itself. "You can't do that," even when we must say it, is often only half the story. "You can't do that *here*, or *now*" is what we really mean. There is usually a way to do it, or a place, or something else that is also enjoyable, and with little effort a mother or father can point it out.[2]

The important subject of growth includes learning self-control and *obedience*. For centuries discipline meant mostly spanking. This is a medieval custom arising out of the sectarian doctrine that because children are born in sin they are born bad. Parents had to spank the badness out of them. Latter-day Saints know that this is not true. One reason for being born into this world is to learn about good and evil.

> Every spirit of man was innocent in the beginning, and God having redeemed man from the fall, men became again, in their infant state, innocent before God." (D&C 93:38.)

Since Satan is not allowed to tempt children before the age of eight, none of what they do could be termed bad or evil. Even when they deliberately defy parents it is only an attempt to find out where the limits stand. Also, children often forget and must be reminded again and again. (And, in our opinion, spanked on occasion.)

Obedience, however, is essential to the growth of children and the peace of mind of adults. The subject is mentioned frequently in the scriptures. "Behold, I, the Lord, utter my voice, and it shall be obeyed." (D&C 63:5.)

"Children, obey your parents in all things: for this is well pleasing unto the Lord." (Col. 3:20.)

In the beginning children obey because their parents require this. Parents, having accumulated a degree of wisdom and good judgment, and being concerned about the welfare of the child, have a right to tell him what to do—and expect him to do it. Indeed it is their responsibility.

---

[2]Sidonie Matsner Gruenberg, *The Parents' Guide to Everyday Problems of Boys and Girls* (New York: Random House, 1958), p. 36.

At the age of two Johnny accepts this because he has faith in his parents. The trust he built during his first year is a base upon which to learn obedience in his second and third years. Without trust, Johnny may already be showing signs of personality disorder. He will cry excessively and acquire an endless repertoire of attention-getting devices, all quite aggravating to his mother. One of these is purposeful disobedience.

Assuming that Johnny does feel trusting and secure, how, then, does a parent or any adult teach him to obey? He is growing and wants to know how important he is compared with everyone else. He wants to know the rules. What can he do safely? What gets him into trouble? The rules should be simple, clear, and consistent.

One good way to teach Johnny at this stage is to demonstrate. Remember that he is just becoming familiar with words, and his vocabulary is quite limited. He is still thinking basically, and too many words confuse him. Telling him to wash his face is all right, but telling him to clean his room is too much without demonstration. Does cleaning a room mean picking up, or making beds, or dusting, or vacuuming? Much childish misbehavior is actually the result of the child's lack of experience or understanding. It is not willful disobedience. Parents need to be sure that Johnny understands what is expected and is shown how to do it.

Once the meaning is clear, the "tell, show, praise" method can be used. If there is a task to be done, tell Johnny *only once*, then take him by the hand and walk him through it step by step. Then praise him for doing it. In this way Johnny learns that he is expected to obey the first time he is told, without mother or father raising their voices. It is also a pleasant experience, for he receives individual attention, feels successful in completing the task, and receives the positive reinforcement of his mother's approval. Mother may then say, "Next time, let's see if you can do it all by yourself." This appeals to his urge to be big and independent.

This method is very time consuming at first, but if it is followed quite consistently, Johnny will very soon learn to obey without a bit of fuss. It will pay big dividends in the future. Discipline will be simpler and easier on everyone's nerves.

Many parents do not expect obedience. Suppose Johnny's mother tells him once and he ignores her. She tells him a second time, with no results. She raises her voice and looks threatening. If he still does not obey she screams at him or spanks him. *She is programming into Johnny's brain that he does not have to obey until she becomes angry.* Discipline then becomes a tug of war between Johnny and his mother to see who can hold out longer. In many homes parents constantly yell at their children and are ignored. This is an unpleasant and frustrating situation that is unnecessary if the children had been properly programmed at age two! The "tell, show, praise" method teaches Johnny that when he is asked to do something, his mother or father expect it to be done and will firmly but kindly insure that the task is accomplished. When it is done they will be happy and will praise him with the same amount of energy they would have used to punish him. An ounce of praise is worth a pound of punishment.

Another gospel principle which applies at all stages of growth is *free agency*. The Lord said, "For behold it is not meet that I should command in all things. . . . For the power is in them wherein they are agents unto themselves." (D&C 58:26, 28.)

Even a two-year-old has free agency, and as soon as he discovers this he becomes very cocky indeed. Immediately this behavior comes into conflict with the principle of obedience. What is the relationship between these two?

To be able to use free agency properly requires wisdom, good judgment, and self-control. At two Johnny doesn't have much of any of these. How will he acquire them? There is another scripture which states, "For he will give unto the faithful line upon line, precept upon precept." (D&C 98:12.)

This means that people must grow one step at a time. Learning obedience first starts Johnny on the path to the self-control which is necessary for the use of free agency. Eventually he should choose to behave in right and proper ways without anyone's standing over him forcing obedience. Even at the age of two, persuading Johnny to do the right thing should be more teaching than forcing. The Savior's way was to lead, to guide, to teach. Joseph Smith once said that he did not attempt to control the people. He taught them right principles and let them govern themselves.

Obviously, at two or three this is often impractical, but it is the goal toward which parents can work. There must be rules which the child understands and which are firmly enforced. (How the Lord uses rewards and punishments will be discussed in chapter 7.)

Learning self control through obedience is the first step to the proper use of free agency. Learning wisdom and good judgment is a second step. This involves partly the acceptance of adult wisdom and partly finding out for oneself through trial and error.

At the age of two Johnny lacks judgment and will make many mistakes. If big brother cuts a piece of cheese, Johnny will imitate without much discretion. Mother is horrified when she sees the knife in Johnny's hand and the cheese on the floor. How, then, do Johnny's parents start him on the long road to good judgment in decision making—the judgment that is necessary for wise use of his free agency? First, they will live and act in such a way that what he imitates is acceptable. Secondly, they will help him to practice making decisions. He learns by doing.

Even a three-year-old may be given some choices, but always within limits. For example, when Johnny is eating breakfast: "Would you like orange juice or pineapple juice?" his mother asks. "I want some cake," he answers.

"Cake is for dessert, Johnny. We'll save that for lunch. Juice helps you grow strong like Dad. It is good for breakfast. Which kind would you like?"

The choice he has been given is one in which either decision will be appropriate. Johnny has the experience of making a successful choice. He also stores away in his brain a bit of wisdom about which foods are appropriate for lunch and which are good for breakfast.

Consider another example. Johnny is dressing to play.

"What would you like to wear today? You may wear these blue jeans and a sweat shirt, or the green pants and T-shirt."

"I want to wear the new suit grandma gave me!"

"Your new suit is too nice to wear just to play in. Let's save it for Sunday School when you will want to look your best for Heavenly Father. Now which outfit do you want?"

Johnny again has had practice in making a successful decision. It was successful because his mother limited the choices to what would be appropriate for the occasion. He has also collected two other bits of wisdom upon which to base future decisions. He learned what kind of clothes are appropriate for play. He learned that Sunday School is a special place where people want to look their best--not for vain reasons but for the Lord.

Every successful decision that Johnny makes programs into his mind a feeling of confidence in his ability to use his own judgment. It helps him build faith in himself. It is important for him to have these choices, within limits, as often as possible while he is growing up. If such a program is followed, when he becomes a teenager he will be making most of his own decisions with good judgment. This enables his parents to have faith in him. He will know that if he has a problem, he can go to them and receive help in considering the pros and cons of the situation. Because they respect his right and ability to make decisions he will be willing to accept information and counsel. Too many children are forced by injured pride and ignorance to make wrong decisions—choices they would make differently if they had had more practice and were not angry with their parents.

How will Johnny be affected if he grows up in a home where parents constantly scream at him, or, when they want him to obey, force him? Two things happen. First, if he obeys at all it will be because he is afraid. This was Lucifer's plan. Parents or teachers help Satan influence their children in later years when force is their *only* method of discipline. As soon as the force is removed, the child does what he wants. He uses his free agency without having first learned wisdom, good judgment, and control. This leaves him open to the influence of Satan. As long as parents are making all the decisions and forcing obedience, Johnny will not be developing in important ways necessary for the later use of his free agency.

At this stage, obedience comes first, but he must also be allowed some choices so that he can start on the long road to mature self direction.

Yelling at children may also mean that the parent is angry. Anger begets fear and anger. Neither is this the Lord's way. Remember the words given to the Priesthood, but applicable to everyone, especially parents:

> No power or influence can or ought to be maintained by virtue of the priesthood, only by persuasion, by long-suffering, by gentleness and meekness, and by love unfeigned;
>
> By kindness, and pure knowledge, which shall greatly enlarge the soul without hypocrisy and without guile. (D&C 121:41-42.)

This kind of self-control is difficult to achieve, especially if one was born with a temper. How much of a sin is it to become angry? If we read the scriptures correctly they say that emotions are natural parts of personality and of life. The Lord himself is angry on occasion. "I, the Lord, was angry with you yesterday, but today mine anger is turned away." (D&C 61:20.)

When things go wrong emotions build up like steam

in a boiler. Many Latter-day Saint parents seem to think they must never show their emotions. They feel like failures because they have a temple marriage and are still short-tempered.

What needs to be learned is that emotions are natural and desirable if controlled. In the scriptures the Lord said he was angry *yesterday*. He had apparently waited a whole day, permitting the anger to subside before he went back and straightened out the problem. Another good scripture is found in Ephesians 4:26-27. "Be ye angry, and sin not: let not the sun go down upon your wrath: Neither give place to the devil."

This scripture explains that the sin is not in becoming angry, but in *staying angry* and in letting the devil make one more angry so that he hurts other people by lashing out at them.

Controlled emotions, however, can be useful. Many a woman has saved her loved ones from danger because of added strength caused by her emotions. Great books have been written because the author was angry about injustice. Powerful testimonies are born by people who are weeping from sorrow or joy. Control makes the difference, but control does not always mean to suppress. Sometimes it means to guide. A baseball pitcher, for example, controls the ball by making it go where he wants it to go. This is what needs to be done with emotions. When used properly they are a valuable gift from the Lord. The Prophet Joseph struck a death blow at the idea that God himself had no "body, parts, or *passions*."

Emotions are part of life, but there is an eternity of difference between a man who calmly says, "That makes me very angry, John" and a man who screams and swears while throwing things at his wife or child. Can you imagine the Savior screaming or swearing, even when he drove the money changers from the temple?

The second result of harsh, unfeeling force is destruction of Johnny's self-respect, and faith in himself. What kind of self-image is programmed into his brain is going to determine to some extent his degree of mental health later on. "Remember the worth of souls is great in the sight of God." (D&C 18:10.) People are important and they must feel that they are. Programming the self-image begins at birth, but becomes most vital during the negative stage. If it is a good image, the child will develop confidence in himself and be able to respect and enjoy other people. If it is a poor image, he will be emotionally crippled, feeling suspicious of others and afraid of himself. He may consider himself unworthy to be loved or even liked by others and will seldom develop his talents enough to earn his own self-respect. Some children become rebellious and fight their parents. Others withdraw within themselves and shut themselves out from the lifegiving, nourishing intermingling of loving spirits. They will be very unhappy persons.

Consider the extreme but pertinent case of Cain. He committed a terrible sin, after which a curse was placed upon him by the Lord. Even though he had committed murder, it seems that his greatest fear was that other people would despise him. He said to the Lord:

> Behold thou hast driven me out this day from the face of the Lord, and from thy face shall I be hid; and I shall be a fugitive and a vagabond in the earth. . . . (Moses 5:39.)

Cain feared what other people would think of him and do to him because within himself he knew what a despicable person he was.

Johnny can survive occasional bursts of unreasonable anger if he knows that his parents love him unconditionally, even when he misbehaves. But under the merciless fire of constant criticism and disapproval, the message finally gets through: "My parents don't like me the way I am. There must be something wrong with me." He may dislike his parents for not understanding that he just wants to grow up and learn to use his free agency. He may resent them for not understanding that he is a child of God, the same as they, meriting respect. Even if he does not show his feelings, the seeds are being sown for trouble later on.

Discipline is necessary, and without it a child will be warped, but the Lord's way is the proper way.

> Reproving betimes with sharpness, when moved upon by the Holy Ghost; and then showing forth afterwards an increase of love toward him whom thou hast reproved, lest he esteem thee to be his enemy;
>
> That he may know that thy faithfulness is stronger than the cords of death. (D&C 121:43-44.)

Take note that one should reprove sharply *when moved upon by the Holy Ghost*, not whenever one becomes angry, or irritated, or tired, and this applies absolutely to Johnny and his parents, his Sunday School and Primary teachers, and all other adults in his life.

Another gospel principle that comes into play at this time is *unity*. The scriptures speak often of having a oneness of purpose, working together and sharing. "And let every man deal honestly, and be alike among this people, and receive alike, that ye may be one, even as I have commanded you." (D&C 51:9.)

Unity should exist in the family as a whole, and especially between husband and wife. With discipline necessary, it is important that mother and dad work as a team. Johnny is smart. If he discovers that when he cannot get what he wants from Dad he can always wheedle it out of Mother, or vice versa, the program in his brain begins to tell him that an effective way to solve life problems is to *use* people. Play them against each other. Flatter them. Tell them anything, true or not, so that they will give him what he wants. People do not like to be used, as Johnny will find out to his sorrow later on.

Unity among family members is also essential to happy family life. Sometimes parents have difficulty in valuing all of their children equally. Children who resemble their father in personality traits, for example, may be easier for him to understand. Their problems will be viewed more sympathetically. He may feel more comfortable around them and spend more time with them. When there are favorites, the family tends to divide into rival camps. Unity is destroyed. Sometimes even the parents are against each other.

The ability to see children as individuals is one of the cornerstones of healthy family life. Every concerned parent should be able to discuss each child's strengths and weaknesses, talents, interests, and personality. It is a danger sign when parents demonstrate ignorance or lack of interest in their individual children. Parents should discuss together regularly the direction of each child's growth. One of the richest experiences of the author was to hear his stake president, in private conversation, analyze each of his ten children. To him they were human beings, brother and sisters, and individuals in the finest sense.

As previously quoted, the worth of souls is great in the sight of God. The Lord loves *all* his children, not just those who are righteous and who please him. So must parents make an effort to value each child for himself, appreciating the good they find in him and helping him to become the best kind of person of which he is capable.

When each child, regardless of age, feels like a valued member of the family, all of them can relate horizontally instead of vertically. No one is worrying about who is older or younger, who is more or less capable. All have good qualities. All have faults. All are growing at their own rates. Even parents. Thus competition is at a minimum and cooperation comes naturally. Unity is achieved. Loving spirits intermingle. The spirit of the Lord feels comfortable in the home.

When Johnny's little sister, Mary, arrives on the scene, jealousy and competition can be kept at a minimum if parents remember to give Johnny some extra attention and help him feel that she is his baby too. The spirit of love and sharing needs to be programmed into Johnny from the first. If he feels that he is a displaced person, less important than his sister, all kinds of annoying attention-getting behavior patterns will result. To reprogram is much more difficult than to teach correctly in the first place.

Letting Johnny hold his baby sister sometimes is a choice experience. He sees how tiny and helpless she is. He sees that she needs people older and bigger to take care of her. Feelings of love awaken. She becomes a valued member of the family.

As any parent knows, each new child presents a challenge. He brings his own special joy, but he also requires more energy, more innovation, more food, and more everything. It is true that parents need to shift gears and adjust. They need proper sleep, recreation, time together, and time with the children. This calls for organization.

With this adjustment they need to think of Mary as more than Johnny's sister. Mary is Mary! She looks different, thinks differently, and will require different approaches. The difference lies in her personality, not in basic, eternally valid principles. Mary needs respect, patience, firmness, love, and the other helps that Johnny needs, but she is a female, and this must be taken into consideration. There are misguided people today trying to destroy the differences between men and women. Attempts to do this will fail because God himself created the sexes, beginning with Adam and Eve. The priesthood is given exclusively to men, and sacred motherhood only to women. Johnny is on the former path and Mary the latter. As they grow up it is important for them to learn about being a boy and being a girl.

One final gospel principle which should begin at this stage is *prayer*, or communication. Children at first have no conception of God. Prayers, therefore, have little meaning when first dutifully repeated after the mother or father. The Lord loves little children, however. His spirit dwells within them, for they are free from sin. The Lord hears and answers their prayers.

Johnny accepts the concept of God first on faith. If he is taught about God and about how to talk to him through prayer, very soon Johnny can gain a personal testimony regarding this.

Many of the children coming into the world these days are the elect of God, the great, strong spirits saved to be born in the last days when Satan would be at the height of his power. Because of their spiritual strength, a beautiful feeling of peace and harmony is felt when they learn about God. The brain is becoming aware of what the spirit already knew. Perceptive adults are sometimes amazed at the intelligent, mature questions asked by young Latter-day Saint children.

Johnny's concept of God, however, will be strongly affected by his relationship with his earthly father. One little boy in Primary seemed puzzled when his teacher described Father in heaven as being loving, kind, and good. She could see that her words were falling on deaf ears. Desiring to understand further she took her problem to the home teachers of this family. What was the boy's father like? He was a tyrant—harsh, angry, unyielding, sometimes drunk. This was what the word *father* meant to this child. The programming in his brain could not reconcile this with a Father in heaven who was just the opposite. Sometimes fathers tragically do not understand how important it is for them to establish a warm, friendly, understanding relationship with their young children.

Prayer is a form of communication, not a ritual. Sometimes, to show young children a picture of Jesus (who resembles his Father) will help them to visualize the person to whom they are praying. It helps them to understand that they are talking to someone who is real. To communicate effectively, children need the assurance that someone is listening when they pray, even though this personage cannot be seen.

Parents, too, need this assurance. Many adults are still repeating ritual prayers they learned as children, or, because these have become meaningless, are not praying at all. How can they teach their children?

To be able to communicate with God, knowing that he is listening and that he can and will answer prayers, is essential to the mental health and well-being of Latter-day Saints. Satan works hard to destroy those who follow Jesus Christ. Without the constant strength and life-giving spirit of the Lord dwelling within, people are open to the buffetings of Satan. The spirit of the Lord cannot, however, dwell in unholy tabernacles. Thus, every parent must seek constantly to live righteously and to learn how to communicate effectively through prayer. And he must teach these to the children.

Parents are entitled to personal revelation and inspiration for the welfare of their families. This is especially true of the father, who, as a priesthood holder, holds the keys to the administration of family affairs. Every Church calling, even those held by women, carries a mantle of authority (delegated by a higher priesthood authority). This entitles them to the personal revelation and guidance necessary to do the Lord's work properly. For Latter-day Saints, raising a family is definitely part of the Lord's work.

At this point it should be evident that the gospel of Jesus Christ is a real and practical guide for the raising of children. Parents need to learn and apply the gospel. If this sounds redundant, remember that Moroni visited Joseph Smith four times in one twenty-four hour period and repeated the same message each time. Parents do not need fancy, complex, ever-changing theories for guidance. They need the eternal principles of the gospel. They need to explore and learn of Heavenly Father's love and of his methods for handling his children. They need gospel discussions and assignments in the Church that keep them in tune with the spirit. They need to learn basic truths and have the joy of applying those truths in specific ways to meet their own family needs.

The Church offers rich resources for the raising of families. The younger Sunday School and Primary classes can be highly effective. These little children need women called as teachers not as baby sitters. The Relief Society nurseries have weekly periods where capable women can influence young children in beneficial ways. Finding intelligent, warm-hearted people for these positions, and giving them technical training in the skills of teaching, will pay dividends to any family or ward.

Active Young Marrieds groups are valuable. These afford opportunities for group discussion and group activity. For more personal talks, couples often visit in each others' homes or go to the bishop. The important factor is that through active, properly correlated groups, struggling young parents with much in common can share views and grow together.

Finances are pertinent at this stage, and the bishop can help these parents learn the great blessings of tithing and proper budgeting either personally or through a qualified ward member.

Family oriented classes in Sunday School are usually well attended because most parents need and seek help with their families. An effective teacher will spread his good influence endlessly through these classes.

Home teachers and Relief Society visiting teachers, carefully assigned, can give wise, experienced counsel and help.

Raising children within The Church of Jesus Christ of Latter-day Saints is a great privilege. Parents must remember the importance of using gospel principles in the basic programming that is occurring during the first few years in their childrens' lives. If Johnny has learned obedience without having his self-respect destroyed and his free agency denied, he will be ready for the next stage in his eternal progression.

Chapter 6

Middle Childhood:
Five Through Seven

Practice Makes Perfect

Chapter 6

Practice Makes Perfect

There is no sharp dividing line between stages of growth. Each child has his own time table so that he goes through the various stages whenever he is ready. Even within the same child, physical growth may be ahead of intellectual achievement, or the social skills may race ahead of spiritual development. In other words, there are different kinds of growth, each with its own time table depending upon opportunity, stimulation, training, aptitude, and other factors.

Growth also is not smooth and steady. It proceeds in a series of spurts and plateaus. Rapid progress in one area may be followed by a period of slower growth in which the child integrates and consolidates the recent rapid gains.

The stage about to be described is, in some respects, like a plateau. Johnny is refining the learnings of earlier stages. To large muscle activities such as running and skipping, he now adds small muscular skills such as coloring, and cutting with scissors. Learning the names of objects is expanded to include having opinions about them.

He is great at asking questions, wanting to know not only "what" but "why" and "how."

Having achieved a measure of competence in handling himself and his little world within the family, Johnny is now ready to reach out tentatively to the larger world. He wants to use his own initiative in finding out about it. Faith in his parents enables him to do this because if he trusts them, he will also trust other children and other adults, particularly teachers. Confidence in his own abilities spurs him on to new conquests.

He discovers that he is like adults in many ways and can do many things that they do. Johnny has visions of growing up to be somebody important, such as a fireman or a television emcee. He is torn between wanting to do big, important things and realizing that in many ways he is still little and incompetent.

This is an age of fantasy in which he often does not know the difference between what is real and what he has made up in his imagination. Parents should not confuse this with lying.

Instead of playing alone, Johnny can now play cooperatively with other children. He can make plans with others and participate in group projects. Responsibility for himself and perhaps for younger brothers and sisters is gradually developing. He has a conscience.

Although Johnny's world is rapidly expanding, his parents are particularly important at this period because they are models of an adult man and an adult woman. As was indicated in the last chapter, for Johnny to develop maleness and Mary to develop femaleness is essential for effective adult functioning and in keeping with the Lord's plan.

This involves more than physical maturation. At about this time, or a little younger, children develop an intense interest in the parent of the opposite sex. Boys are very attached to their mothers. Girls are fascinated by their strong, handsome fathers. Each may be jealous of anyone who interferes with this relationship. Parents need to recognize this and devote extra time and attention to children of the opposite sex—play with them, talk to them, listen to them, teach them, answer their questions, hold them on their laps, be physically affectionate.

If Johnny has developed into a strong, confident person, he will go through this period quite rapidly. If previous programming has been faulty he may want to relive what he missed earlier by seeking to perpetuate an infantile, dependent attachment to his mother. This interferes with his ability to get close to his father and become like him.

For Mary to continue in an infantile, dependent role means that she will have difficulty becoming an independent, strong person in her own right. It may also interfere with the warm, close relationship she needs to experience with her father. This will be a handicap later in her feelings about boys. Many teenage unwed mothers have disturbed relationships with their fathers. When any boy says "I love you" it unlocks all the pent-up unsatisfied emotions that she has carried about since childhood. The emotional hunger is so great that the feelings easily get out of control.

Assuming that the programming has been skillful to this point, Johnny will soon turn his attention back to his father and decide that he wants to be like him. Mary will turn from her father back to her mother and start learning how to be a woman.

Both parents then become models and prototypes strongly affecting the future relationships between the sexes. It is an understatement to say that sex plays an important part in the development of human personality. It is so important, in fact, that the Lord has given very specific guidelines concerning sexual behavior. These guidelines are for the benefit of both parents and children. One of the greatest truths about human behavior is that the sexual attitudes of the parents affect the lives of their offspring for generations—not just physically, but morally, emotionally, and spiritually.

In real fact, if Johnny's father exercises his priesthood righteously and sincerely, then Johnny and Mary have an ideal example of manhood in action. This same principle holds true as Johnny's mother honors her husband and honors her own role as a woman, mate, and mother.

To follow this idea through, observe Johnny in situations which are common to five-year-old boys. At this stage, Johnny is still attached strongly to his parents. From them he learns how to love, to trust, and to handle his emotions. Johnny is struggling to find out just who he is and what it means to be a male. His parents help him in many ways. His mother's attitude may say, "What a nice big boy you are. You are kind, considerate, and loyal, just like your father whom I love." His father imparts to the boy a respectful, healthy attitude toward women because of the way he treats Johnny's mother. He is also proud of Johnny, and secure enough to give him a good part of his life because he loves him. Johnny is then started on the road to a healthy concept of himself and his sexual identity. Healthy programming is going on in this part of his brain.

On the other hand, suppose Johnny's mother finds it necessary to protect him from a father whose idea of masculinity is to be agressive, harsh, and disrespectful. Johnny may become confused because mother is nicer, and he knows that he is a man, and men (his father) are bullies. For him to want to identify with such a father is unlikely. The programming in his brain will be out of harmony with the spirit, which knew from personal experience a kind and loving Heavenly Father in its premortal existence. This means trouble for Johnny.

Suppose his mother is also an angry, irritable, unloving type, while his father is seldom at home (probably to avoid his wife). The hurt caused by mother and the lack of a **suitable masculine example** may result in

Johnny's disliking women. When he becomes a teenager, he may be still treating all women as if they were his unpleasant mother, so that he either fears them or fights them. He may use sex to exploit women and so overpower them. His chances for a happy marriage are slim.

Sometimes, however, a boy such as this will still be looking for the loving mother he never knew. He will be attracted to older girls who are very sympathetic and maternal. If he marries one of these he will have difficulty functioning as a husband and father. He will be like a child. Without drastic reprogramming on his part, such a marriage will be unsatisfactory at best.

How about Mary and her concept of femininity? Her father's attitude says to Mary, "You are a beautiful little girl. I respect you because I respect women and have an assurance of my own manhood. I do not need to swear, drink, and be rough to feel like a man." Mary's mother, not by so many words but by countless impressions accumulated over the years, passes her attitudes to Mary that marriage is a natural expression of love between responsible, considerate partners. Homemaking is enjoyable. To be a wife and mother is a great and noble calling.

What if Mary's father teaches her that as a female she is only something to be used and discarded—treating her and her mother well only when he wants something? Mary's eternal spirit and her mortal brain must come into severe conflict in this situation. Tenderness, kindness, and love surely characterized her premortal spiritual experiences.

For a woman to be abused sexually is one of the most vile crimes against free agency. One of the most common abuses occurs when a man expects sexual activity no matter how he has treated his wife that same day. Too many men will turn from a bitter argument with their wives and expect them to engage in sexual relations without any intervening reconciliation. They seem to separate the sex act from love, and in doing so strike a major blow to their wives' self respect. Such behavior eventually destroys the marriage—and often the woman's emotional health. To teach it to Mary or John is devastating.

The subject of sex education is confusing to many Latter-day Saint parents, mostly because the word *sex* is so distorted in worldly cultures and because for most people the word creates strong, embarrassing emotional reactions. In the Lord's scheme of things men and women each have their distinct functions and responsibilities. Sexuality, in the larger context, simply means that men and women each perform the tasks and assume the responsibilities of the particular sex to which they belong.

Procreation is only one part of sexuality. Perhaps the Lord made it particularly enjoyable so that human beings will not frustrate the plans of God for his children by losing interest in the whole thing. Few mortals realize, however, what a great privilege it is to have sex relations. Those who abuse the privilege stand in danger of losing it completely for all eternity. After this life, only the very few who reach the highest degree of the celestial kingdom will be granted the opportunity of eternal procreation.

> . . . And they shall pass by the angels, and the Gods, which are set there, to their exaltation and glory in all things, as hath been sealed upon their heads, which glory shall be a fullness and a continuation of the seeds forever and ever. (D&C 132:19.)

No wonder that Satan, who will never have this experience, uses sexual impurity to drag as many as possible down to degradation. His message comes through loud and clear these days.

Television and movies expose children to all sorts of adult information at an early age. Naturally they are curious. Johnny cannot be protected from all the evil in the world, but he can be taught the truth about it. His parents should know what he is seeing and hearing so that they can help him evaluate it. If he can talk honestly with his parents, he will be less likely to believe the distorted information which he will hear elsewhere. The discussion should always emphasize sexuality in its broad, spiritual context.

When Johnny utters a four letter word that he has picked up at school or at play, it could be a shock to his parents and teachers, especially if he does it in Primary class. Often a parent will surprise Johnny and his playmates as the children are exploring each others' genitals. This is unsettling to parents who place a high premium on moral standards. Experience has shown that the worst way to handle these incidents is to get excited. Life-long scars have been left by parents who have over-reacted. To be screamed at or called a "filthy little thing" devastates the child. Into his brain is burned an image of worthlessness that is most difficult to reprogram. He believes that his genitals and his sexuality are somehow unclean and to be condemned. This is not true, else why would the Creator design the body so?

Those parents who have weathered these experiences successfully have done so by explaining calmly that such exposure is not proper and by diverting the child's attention to other pursuits. The goal is the same as with the excited parents, but the quiet method keeps the issue in perspective.

Actually, there are two parts to sex education. One is specifically biological and refers to conception of babies, menstrual periods, puberty, etc. If Johnny does not ask questions, pets are helpful. The differences between animals and people, however, should be emphasized. Animals mate indiscriminately. Being human means that the Lord expects people to live higher laws.

The physical aspects are usually taught at school in biology and health classes. Children should know about body processes by the time they are ten years old. This does not happen all at once, but step by step as his curiosity is aroused and as he is able to understand. This may sound young, but some girls become pregnant by the time they are twelve or thirteen.

The other part of the sex question refers to moral behavior. Some children never learn anything beyond the physical aspects of sex. Herein lies the danger. As has been indicated, Johnny needs to learn strong moral values in his own home by watching how his father and mother treat each other. He needs to know about spiritual sexuality (as described above) before being exposed to the biological information.

So, at ages five through seven sex education means answering Johnny's questions honestly, letting his dog have puppies, and raising him in a moral home where father and mother are setting good examples of masculinity and feminity. They need to understand the gospel principles of modesty, chastity and love. When parents dress and behave modestly, they automatically teach Johnny that men and women have a respected private body that very few people ever see and only one other person ever touches intimately. The beauty and uniqueness of sex is enhanced by modesty in a way that the world, obviously, cannot even imagine. Unfortunately, many Latter-day Saints do not comprehend this either. Immodesty, especially to the extreme point of permitting children to observe sexual relations, is destructive and can result in severe personality problems.

Along with modesty goes chastity. This refers to the preservation of sexual intimacy for one's spouse. It should be enough to say, as Adam, "I know not, save I was commanded." Fortunately, the blessings of chastity are known to concerned parents, and Johnny needs to learn them now. He sees and hears his parents give their attention and affection only to each other as they hold hands or embrace. An understanding of chastity begins at age three or four—not at age thirteen or fourteen.

As modesty and chastity are eternal principles, so is love. There is damage in a family where appropriate affection is never seen by children. Love at this point in the discussion refers to affection between **men** and women rather than between parents and children. Johnny's parents, because they know the gospel, do not hide their love or deny it. They show appropriate affection in front of Johnny as they embrace. They speak of it. The "real thing" is both spiritual and physical, permitted by a marriage covenant and sanctfied by personal relationships between people who love each other deeply.

This discussion is an oversimplification of a very complex subject. Parents need to keep in mind, however, that they are the models for their children's attitudes toward moral behavior and sex identity.

Another important principle of the gospel of Jesus Chirst is *intelligence, the light of truth,* or education. This is a difficult subject for mortals to understand, since the word *intelligence* means something far more to the Lord than what is measured by an I.Q. test. Nevertheless, Latter-day Saints stress the importance of education. The prophet Joseph Smith was told,

Teach ye diligently and my grace shall attend you, that you may be instructed more perfectly in theory, in principle, in doctrine, in the law of the gospel, in all things that pertain unto the kingdom of God, that are expedient for you to understand;

Of things both in heaven and in the earth, and under the earth; things which have been, things which are, things which must shortly come to pass; things which are at home, things which are abroad; the wars and perplexities of the nations, and the judgments which are upon the land; and a knowledge also of countries and of kingdoms. (D&C 88:78-79.)

Five-year-old Johnny is getting ready to go to school. What will this mean to him? Most children are eager to start kindergarten, but by the time they are in the second or third grade some of them will be disillusioned because the work is too difficult or the teacher unsympathetic or unskilled. Sometimes the child himself has trouble adjusting to school.

Already, faulty programming may be evident through behavior problems. Johnny is now in competition with other children. A good image of himself is important, for he must feel that he is as capable as other children, at least in some ways. Failure to meet the demands of the school situation may discourage and handicap him throughout life. He may be a potential drop-out, and can often be spotted in the first or second grade.

As a negative example, meet Robert M., who at nineteen was asked by his mother and step-father to leave home. His problem developed at age five because of misunderstanding and the failure of adults to be perceptive.

Robert was born in Los Angeles to an active LDS couple who had no other children. He fell and struck his head at age three. At age five in kindergarten his teacher, with whom he had several disagreements, said that he was mildly retarded according to an I.Q. test. It was assumed that his earlier fall had resulted in brain damage. This report was on his record and went unchallenged the rest of his school career. His parents, from a mixture of love and fear at this so-called defect in their only child, began treating him as some people treat a retarded person, tending to expect little of him and protecting him from many ordinary life experiences.

When Robert was eight his parents divorced, and his mother remarried the following year. This new arrangement left Robert without much companionship. He was tolerated. He managed to graduate from high school at eighteen, but was so rude and irresponsible that he was thrown out of the family home. The bishop took him in tow and sent him to an LDS social worker for evaluation.

It was an unsettling interview, because the social worker felt strongly that Robert was not mentally retarded. Subsequent psychological testing confirmed that Robert's mental equipment was actually a bit above average. The tragedy, though, was that his parents' treatment and that of his teachers had so warped him that he was socially and emotionally retarded. In other words, his brain was fine, but his behavior, maturity, and personality had developed to meet only the expectations of those adults who considered him mentally retarded. As seen by his high school diploma he could achieve, so there was hope.

The bishop in this case took five major steps. The first, already mentioned, was to arrange a thorough physical and psychological examination for Robert. This examination confirmed the social worker's feeling that Robert was not mentally retarded.

Second, he helped Robert find a home with an older couple. These fine Latter-day Saint people undertook to help Robert so that he could relearn many social and emotional patterns in a mature way (reprogram faulty brain patterns). It was virtually fruitless to worry about the past so they concentrated primarily on his present needs.

Third, the bishop helped him find a job that was within his capacity and which had a future. Robert's new employer quite enjoyed the opportunity to help him.

Fourth, the bishop apprised Robert's priests quorum advisor of the problem (with Robert's permission), and the advisor helped Robert grow through Church activity and companionship.

Fifth, Robert's mother and step-father were called in by the bishop and enlisted in the effort, mainly through providing financial help to Robert while he was getting established. They had developed habitual responses to Robert's so-called handicap, so it was decided by all concerned that Robert's best hope for recovery lay independent of them.

While Robert's improvement was gradual, it was sure, and the time came when he was able to enter adult life and build for himself.

As in Robert's case, while school is critically important, parents are the key to healthy development during this period. Some of them want to shift the full responsibility to the teacher, but those who remember that the child is a great spirit struggling with his eternal progression will want to do all they can to encourage him and to help him feel competent.

A home environment that includes books, music, art, and stimulating conversation is most helpful. Part of the family home evening can occasionally be devoted to nature walks or to finding answers in the encyclopedia. This atmosphere carries over to school.

Leaving the relatively calm atmosphere of home to enter the much more complex environment of school causes new stresses on Johnny. If he is reasonably self-assured, if his experiences with adults have been warm and consistent, and if he is armed with an understanding of basic moral behavior, school can be an exciting new adventure.

For some children, the first adult with whom they really spend much time, other than father and mother, is their teacher. If that teacher is a friend, then Johnny is fortunate. The alternative should be obvious. A sensitive teacher can tell which children have been taught to obey, which ones have never had to share, which ones are hungry for love and affection. Schools do what they can to correct deficiencies, but it is not fair—or wise—to expect teachers always to succeed where parents have failed.

To think of intelligence and the light of truth only in terms of school education is a mistake. Growth in intelligence means growth of the spirit on all fronts. It means learning about the gospel truths from the scriptures. It means drawing close to the Lord so that the Holy Ghost can bear testimony to what is true and what is false. It means increasing the ability of the spirit to control the body—especially the brain—and to achieve an eventual harmony between the two. It means learning also from experience, and from the experiences of others. Formal schooling is important, but to equate this with education is taking a very narrow view.

Johnny is now approaching the age of accountability. Part of his education should include preparation for baptism. A family home evening should be devoted to the subject. Primary and Sunday School classes also help with this.

Teachers in these classes can also help in other ways. If he seeks attention, they need to give it to him, appropriately. Assignments, challenges, and warm hugs are better than rebukes. He is also competing with other children at public and at church school. He needs support, more so if it is lacking at home. He needs to succeed at some things and fail honestly at others. Failure can be a teachable moment when Johnny can learn to correct mistakes and to go on to new successes. He should never be ridiculed.

If Johnny's bishop were to visit his Sunday School or Primary class he would see demonstrations of the problems and strengths of the families in his ward. Real prevention is possible at this stage through alert Church workers. What if the problem is the Primary president's son? Is it worth his salvation to ignore it? Are not the monthly oral evaluations for the purpose of helping all Church members in their family units? Such a situation needs to be approached tactfully, but parents who are honestly concerned will welcome all the help they can get.

These years from five through seven provide the final opportunity of Johnny's parents to teach him without interference from Satan. Johnny's basic programming is almost complete. Personality patterns are pretty well formed. The habits, attitudes, and values of the parents have been mostly absorbed.

By the age of eight Johnny should have faith in himself, faith in his parents, and faith in God. He should be making good progress in the use of his free agency so that he does many good things of his own accord without having to be told. There should be a unity and rapport among family members so that Johnny feels that he belongs and is a valued and respected member of the group, as are all the others regardless of age. Obedience should not be a big problem, since he learned long ago that his parents will not ask him to do anything unreasonable and that what they do ask must be done. If he questions, he knows his parents will explain in terms that he can understand.

This is the ideal. Obviously parents are going to make some mistakes and should not feel guilty because they haven't yet reached perfection. If parents love their children and respect them as individuals, the children will weather all kinds of storms and come through pretty well. The more skilled they are, however, the better will be Johnny's chances of reaching adulthood as a mature, competent human being.

Chapter 7

Pre-Adolescence: Eight Through Twelve

The Age of Accountability

Chapter 7

The Age of Accountability

Johnny's eighth birthday is a turning point in his life. He can now be baptized and receive the Holy Ghost. He can commit sin. He is accountable for his actions in an eternal way. These differences are not immediately apparent after baptism, however. He still looks like the same little boy.

During these pre-adolescent years his physical growth slows somewhat while he consolidates his previous gains and prepares for a new spurt of growth which will come near the end of this period. He has an overwhelming urge to practice and acquire competence, especially in manual skills.

In basic and permanent ways Johnny is turning into an adult. His coordination improves; he likes team sports, model building, and collecting. Johnny's sister may become very interested in cooking and other creative aspects of homemaking. This is the golden age for teaching household skills. Real work begins to take the place of play and pretending. Socially, boys like to be with other boys; girls like other girls. The competition, teasing, and apparent friction **between the sexes** means only that Johnny knows the girls are there but doesn't feel quite comfortable around them. The girls are developing faster than Johnny, and they also are ill at ease.

Competition with brothers and sisters subsides somewhat, but the competition in the peer groups is keen. To avoid programming inferiority feelings, Johnny must feel that he can hold his own among his friends.

In some ways this phase of growth is like the month of March, except that it comes in like a lamb and goes out like a lion. At eight children are usually quite tractable and cooperative. At twelve they may seem to turn into monsters. They are cocky, irresponsible, and careless in personal appearance. Fighting and quarreling seem never to end. One parent described this as the "grouchy stage." What has happened?

These are symptoms or changes which can lead to healthy independence or unhealthy rebellion. Johnny is leaving his own baby self behind. He is telling his parents and teachers that he wants to grow up. He wants them to stop treating him as they did when he was three or four. He wants new responsibilities and new privileges. He wants adults to respect him and his ideas and to trust him.

Almost all parents misunderstand these symptoms. They are seen as threats to parental authority instead of indications of healthy growth. When Johnny's behavior is feared as symptoms of predelinquency, his parents panic and crack down. They go back to the two-year-old stage and demand strict obedience. What happens? Johnny's God-given free agency is being threatened, although he may not think of it in these terms. His eternal progression is being thwarted by his own parents. No wonder he resists. The more harsh and strict the discipline, the more difficult Johnny becomes. Remember that inside his growing body is an eternal spirit created by, and subject to, unchanging laws of God, one of which is that individuals progress eternally. To attempt to block progression violates these laws.

The answer to all this is to help him earn the right to feel grown up and responsible. If he knows that mother and dad understand his need for new, more adult experiences and challenges, his cocky, rebellious behavior will eventually turn into confident, helpful behavior. If he is treated like a four-year-old, he will continue to struggle rebelliously on up into the teen years. Eventually and inevitably a break away from authority will come, to everyone's sorrow.

Some adults still show the scars of battles lost in their preteen years. Some become timid and withdrawn; others rebel. Those children who submit docilely to overprotection at this stage fail to develop into strong, independent personalities. Some girls get married not knowing how to handle household responsibilities. A twenty-year-old girl, for example, was afraid to call her doctor for an appointment. "My mother always did that for me," she said.

Grown men leave clothes lying around, still expecting to be waited on hand and foot. Some turn into henpecked husbands because they have never learned to assert themselves in cooperative ways. They feel inferior, and their wives despise them for it.

Children who become rebellious at being thwarted in their growth find themselves in all kinds of trouble with their parents and the law. Some become delinquents, and later, criminals. Others, as the years stretch ahead, drive themselves ruthlessly to get to the top in the business or professional world, regardless of who gets hurt and how sharp or even dishonest the business practices. Often it is their own wives and children who are hurt worst. The father's drive to prove to the world that he is a worthwhile person, worthy of respect, takes precedence over everything. If he can achieve this by the time he is a teenager, how much happier he and his future family will be.

Few parents understand how crucial is this pre-adolescent stage. Not until their sons or daughters are in trouble as teenagers do they realize that something has gone wrong. By then it is too late to do anything but re-program—if they know how, and if the son or daughter will let them.

As mentioned before, the key word for this age is *practice*. Johnny is trying out what had been learned during his eight years of programming. He is also moving ahead in some areas. Great self-confidence is derived from learning manual skills. If he has no work to do, no new skills to learn, he will remain awkward and feel unsure of himself. He needs to compete successfully with his friends so that his confidence and self-respect will grow enough to fight the adult battles that lie ahead. He does not need to succeed in everything. Even one well-developed skill will be a lifelong asset.

The Savior gave a great key to mental health in his parable of the talents, referring to both money and skills.

> For the kingdom of heaven is as a man traveling into a far country, who called his own servants, and delivered unto them his goods.
>
> And unto one he gave five talents, to another two, and to another one; to every man according to his several ability; and straightway took his journey.
>
> After a long time the lord of those servants cometh, and reckoneth with them.
>
> And so he that had received five talents came and brought other five talents, saying, Lord, thou deliveredst unto me five talents: behold, I have gained beside them five talents more.
>
> His lord said unto him, Well done, thou good and faithful servant: thou hast been faithful over a few things, I will make thee ruler over many things: enter thou into the joy of thy lord.
>
> Then he which had received the one talent came and said, Lord, I knew thee that thou art an hard man. . . .
>
> And I was afraid, and went and hid thy talent in the earth: lo, there thou hast that is thine.
>
> His lord answered and said unto him, Thou wicked and slothful servant. . . .
>
> Thou oughtest therefore to have put my money to the exchangers, and then at my coming I should have received mine own with usury.
>
> Take therefore the talent from him, and give it unto him which hath ten talents.

THE AGE OF ACCOUNTABILITY

For unto every one that hath shall be given, and he shall have abundance: but from him that hath not shall be taken away even that which he hath.

And cast ye the unprofitable servant into outer darkness; there shall be weeping and gnashing of teeth. (Math. 25:14, 15, 19-21, 24-30.)

As is so vividly stated in this scripture, the development of skills and abilities of all sorts is an important principle with the Lord because he knows the joy and self-confidence that growth can give to his children. A wise parent will help Johnny explore his world successfully and will see that he has work to do at home, although mother or father can often do a job easier and faster alone. Patience is required to let Johnny and his sister learn, but it is a parent's responsibility to so teach. It is important for Johnny to do *well* whatever he does and to complete what he starts. Only then can he feel pride in his accomplishments and feel good about himself. In this way one of the great patterns of any truly happy life is formed—the ability to enjoy work.

Young Bruce H., from age eight through twelve, had a difficult time. His story personifies the problems that can develop at this stage and affect later years.

Bruce's father was a very capable but insecure man. He did well in high school but never went to college, mainly for financial reasons. He always felt he was undertrained for his potential. Bruce's mother was even more capable than his father but left college after one semester due to lack of self-confidence and money. They met and were married at ages twenty-three and twenty-one respectively.

His parents were active in the Church and were married in the temple. Bruce was born one year later. His sister was born two years after him. Bruce's father was a clerk in a store until his ambitious effort secured a job with a company that required a move from their small community to a large west coast city. The pressures of the move weighed heavily on Bruce's parents, since they were leaving all their family, friends, and familiar surroundings.

As Bruce passed into his sixth year he began school, infected by his parent's insecurities. He thought he looked funny, and he had little self-confidence. He had a very quick mind which, at this stage, caused him difficulty because in quite innocent ways he made rather frank comments to his playmates and teachers. He also had a slight hearing problem that made it difficult to hear his teachers unless he was close. Unfortunately, his quick tongue, plus his lack of self-confidence, caused him to seek attention in annoying ways which prompted his teachers to banish him to the back of the room where he heard even less.

A further problem arose from his training, which, as his parents saw it, forbade fighting, even in self-defense. Being timid anyway, he soon became the neighborhood punching bag. If he had not been fairly large, the situation might have been worse.

All this was not so crucial because until this time he had had substantial emotional support from the basic love in his home. He relied heavily on his parents. What really began to hurt was that his efforts to grow up at age eight through twelve were misunderstood and criticized by his parents. Being their first child, Bruce was a special challenge anyway. His superior mind caused him to explore areas of behavior that upset his parents. He was not cruel or violent, just unusual. For example, he let his mind wander one day (as it often did) during family prayer and he began to hum a time. After the prayer ended, his mother, in confused indignation, angrily grabbed him and shook him, demanding to know what was wrong with him. As an isolated incident this was not significant, but unfortunately it characterized his parents' attitude for the next several years. They frequently demanded that he explain what was wrong with him. He eventually began to wonder the same thing, but did not know the answer.

Since these should have been practice years, Bruce needed to learn many things. His parents, however, were very busy. His father was building a career, and his mother gave birth to two more children. Bruce never developed one skill that gave him an exciting and confident feeling of success. His bright intellect led him to be interested in many subjects, but his immature body could not handle manual tasks. Dad did not help because of his work schedule. Besides, neither dad nor mother had enough confidence to teach him anyway.

By the time Bruce became a teenager, he was badly damaged—not because of vicious physical mistreatment, but because he had virtually no self-confidence or skills. He failed some subjects in junior high and received A's in others. He began to smoke and violate the Sabbath. He left MIA and eventually quit the Boy Scouts. He "borrowed" cars. He failed an entire grade. He began to date at fourteen and was physically intimate with girls, although he did not engage in sexual intercourse. In most ways his life was headed downhill. He was not a good Latter-day Saint, nor was he a healthy human being. The point here is that his problems did not originate in his teens; they only became obvious then. The origin lay in those years from eight to twelve, and earlier.

Then things began to change. In spite of everything, Bruce's parents loved him. The power of unselfish love must never be underestimated. Even though they did not understand him, they never rejected him. His parents were not very skillful, but they stuck by him.

A series of bishops took him to heart. They did not spend much time with him, but he could go to them when necessary. Once he broke a church window by accident. He was extremely fearful that the bishop would be angry— just like mother and dad. A marvelous new world opened to him when the bishop complimented him for being honest in reporting the accident and helped him devise a plan for repayment. Things began to look up.

Later, another bishop made a point of shaking his hand every Sunday and complimenting him whenever possible on his good behavior.

Many other crucial experiences led to Bruce's rehabilitation, all of which involved patient adults. A Sunday School teacher saw his potential and gave him the spotlight whenever possible. He began to taste the joy of success, eventually becoming one of the class leaders.

An explorer leader took him through to real achievement and the development of skills. At school a counselor spent many hours listening and talking. All of these people treated Bruce like someone worthwhile.

Church athletics helped as he made friends and gained some self-esteem.

Then one day a golden experience occurred. He and some friends were picked up by the authorities for an illegal act. After being booked and released pending final action and having nowhere to go he took his friends to his father's office. When they told their story, his father came through like a professional. He was calm, understanding, even a little funny. Bruce's life took a major upswing, even though he had to be punished.

He eventually served a mission, went to college, married in the temple, and was active in the Church. He still fights the effects of his treatment during the years from eight to twelve and has self doubts, but he is, on the whole, a happy and healthy person.

All the ingredients for life-long misery were present in this case, but thanks to Church workers and other concerned adults doing their duty in the spirit of love, Bruce was literally saved from a miserable life. The experiences he missed in childhood were lost, but successful reprograming took place when he focused on the here and now. He developed self-respect, self-confidence, and a strong conscience later in life than desirable, but still soon enough to salvage him from a wasted life.

A second look should now be taken at the subject of

discipline. Some people think of this only as punishment. A better view is "training that corrects, molds, or perfects the mental faculties or moral character." (Webster.) This involves control. It may or may not involve punishment. Always the goal is to shift control from the parents to the children as rapidly as they become responsible and are able to control themselves.

In chapter 5 it was noted that obedience must be learned first, while Johnny is gaining the wisdom, knowledge, and self-discipline to use his free agency wisely. If this was well-learned as a preschooler, Johnny will be ready by the age of accountability to be trusted to make quite a few decisions for himself, which is what he wants.

If he did not learn these lessons, he will turn into a headstrong, unmanageable boy. Reprograming is particularly difficult because, as has been explained, children already tend to be somewhat headstrong at this time. Even under the best of circumstances, Johnny still lacks judgment in many areas. Limits must still be placed upon some of his choices.

Another influence, however, is beginning to have a strong effect upon his decision-making. Johnny is developing a moral code in which all the world is divided into two camps—good and bad, right and wrong. Later he will discover that there is a gray area and that decisions are not that simple. At eight or nine, however, he usually wants to be on the right side but needs parents to help him see the right and remain firm in his decisions. Satan's influence is beginning to complicate matters further. One way parents can help Johnny is by the use of appropriate rewards and punishments, which assist in clarifying the good-bad issues.

Observe how Heavenly Father disciplines his children. Remember the Beatitudes? "Blessed are the meek: for they shall inherit the earth." "Blessed are the pure in heart: for they shall see God." These are rewards for good behavior. Obedience to law earns a reward in God's kingdom.

The scriptures also teach that, "Wickedness never was happiness" and "The wages of sin is death." All through the scriptures the Lord makes very clear the rewards for righteousness and the punishment for sin. As Father in heaven uses rewards and punishment, so can Johnny's parents. The important issue is that Johnny knows ahead of time what the reward will be if he does his assigned tasks and what the punishment will be if he refuses. This permits him to use his free agency. He can choose whether to do the right thing and reap the reward, or to do wrong and take the consequences. If he chooses the latter, parents must accept this. He must be permitted to make mistakes sometimes so he can learn through his own experience. If parents become angry, this gives him a chance to argue and accuse mom or dad of being mean. Parents then get trapped into a battle of wills, and emotions hide the real issue.

As an example, suppose Johnny likes to have his friend over in the evening, but has trouble getting his homework done. His parents may tell him that if his homework is done by dinner time, his friend may come to visit. If the homework is not done, the friend may not come. Of course other factors are involved. Homework is difficult. Parents need to help Johnny study properly; they should take into account the need for privacy, quiet, equipment, and working space. Johnny may want to obey, but if other conditions are negative he may fail in spite of his desires. Nevertheless, if he chooses not to do the homework, the prescribed consequences must follow.

Actually, all acts carry their own rewards or punishments, but these are sometimes not clearly seen. Immediate results may be pleasant, but the long range consequence tragic. Smoking and having cancer might be an example of this. At this age, "good" and "bad" need to be clear, and the reward or punishment swift and meaningful. This is why parents sometimes need to *impose* a punishment.

Later, when Johnny matures, he should be willing to

discipline himself because he can see the natural good results of actions such as doing his homework. He then does the right thing because he can see the value of it and because he *wants* to. When Johnny reaches this level of self-discipline, his parents can trust him more and more to make his own decisions. His errors will be innocent mistakes, not deliberate misbehavior.

There are times, of course, when Johnny *is* deliberately contrary. The wrong act is performed before any rewards or punishments have been explained. For effective moral programming, misbehavior must result in some kind of unpleasant consequence. If the natural results have already frightened or hurt him, then no additional punishment needs to be imposed because he has already learned his lesson in the best possible way. If he has *enjoyed* the misbehavior, then his parents must do two things. First, they must explain what is wrong with what has been done. Second, they must impose a punishment directly connected with the misdeed.

For example, if he breaks a lamp, he must earn the money to replace it, or, if it was a very expensive lamp, at least part of the money. This applies to children of all ages. If a four-year-old writes on the wall, he can be required to help clean the wall. A group of teenage pranksters can be required to wash a store window after having marked it up with soap.

One of the hardest ordeals for parents is to watch their children suffer for their misdeeds. This is what Heavenly Father does, however. Seeing his children suffer does not make him happy, but they must learn to use their free agency—the hard way if necessary. "Verily, thus saith the Lord unto you whom I love, and whom I love I also chasten that their sins may be forgiven, for with the chastisement I prepare a way for their deliverance...." (D&C 95:1.)

Remember that Heavenly Father has given to his children the eternal principle of repentance. If a person is truly sorry for what he has done and has made proper restitution, the Lord will forgive and forget. "Behold, he who has repented of his sins, the same is forgiven, and I, the Lord, remember them no more." (D&C 58:42.)

So it must be with Johnny. If he is truly sorry he should be forgiven.

Repentance, however, involves more than just being sorry. If he goes no further in the process he will carry within him an uncomfortable load of guilt which, if compounded endlessly, destroys self-respect. Besides being sorry and forsaking the undesirable behavior, he must also *make restitution* as best he can for what he has done.

This is why the punishment needs to be directly connected with the offense. It will give Johnny a chance to erase his guilt by making right what he has done wrong. Spanking is likely to stop the misbehavior but it is not enough. He may be sorry only that he was apprehended as the culprit. This is how many young people, and indeed adults, have developed the philosophy that "anything goes as long as you don't get caught." The God-given conscience may be lulled into inertia.

Some people claim that the way to avoid destructive guilt feelings is to say that there is no right or wrong. The Lord, however, is very clear on this point. There definitely is a strong moral code, but this does not mean that wrongdoers need to live with guilt. If they complete the *entire* repentance process, including restitution, guilt feelings will be dissipated in the knowledge that they have atoned for their sin and their Heavenly Father has forgiven them. If he can do this, then they should be able to forgive themselves.

As soon as Johnny arrives at the age of accountability, the repentance process should be part of his every-day living experience. The word *repent* need not be used, as it sometimes has a negative connotation meaning "you are a bad person." In correcting children a distinction should always be made between the unacceptable act and the child, who is still loved and respected as a person. He should never be made to feel that he is hopelessly bad. The *principle* of repentance, however, can be practiced with every misbehavior. A boy or girl who grows up knowing how to deal with guilt feelings by showing he is sorry and making restitution as best he can will likely become a very healthy person mentally.

Many adults have committed and confessed to sins but still cannot live with themselves because they need the purifying experience of making some sort of restitution.

Criminals sometimes give themselves up to the law so that they will be punished. Their load of guilt is too heavy to carry. People have been known to make martyrs of themselves unnecessarily because their consciences were bothering them. Their punishment is self-inflicted. How much more effective it would have been to deal with the problem immediately, going to the persons who have been hurt and smoothing out the differences, paying the debt, or repairing the damage.

When proper restitution has been made and they know they have been forgiven, peace does come. This does not mean, however, that a person will ever *forget* the bad mistakes he made, nor should he. To remember is to learn from the experience and not repeat it. This, too, is part of repentance.

Not much has been said about Mary in this stage. All the general principles which have been discussed apply also to her. One special phenomenom, however, is worthy of comment. She is developing faster than Johnny and is more mature. The differences will be most noticeable between the ages of about ten and fourteen. Mary may also mature faster than some of her girl friends. If she does, great care needs to be taken to help her not to feel self-conscious and conspicuous. If Johnny is small for his age, he too will need similar reassurance.

Physically, Mary must receive instruction about her changing body. Mother and dad have this great privilege. They can take her aside, perhaps pray together, and then discuss in clean, refined, modest, and correct terms what is occurring within her and what the future holds. When she gets older, other aspects of the matter can be explained. She will then be prepared for the onslaughts of the world. There is no mightier weapon than truth.

Latter-day Saints have been thoroughly warned by the Lord's spokesmen that sex instruction belongs in the home. This is so! If parents fail, children are left defenseless and confused, with misinformation bombarding them on all sides.

By now it should be apparent that the age of accountability is a critical crossroads in Johnny's life. Healthy practice of correct principles during the years from eight through twelve is absolutely essential to stable adult life. In adulthood the individual is just an older version of this period of life. Many people never change much after these years. This is where the sheep and the goats seem to part ways.

Fortunately, as with all other periods of life, the Church can be a strength and support to parent and child. Education in gospel principles is essential. Parents who know how to apply these in rearing their children can solve most of their problems, providing their own immaturities are not too disabling.

The Church has unparalleled resources to help Johnny and Mary. Primary activities can teach boys about work and achievement. Girls' programs in the Primary and MIA are equally effective. Sunday School lessons must be not only idealistic but practical and useful in their lives.

Home teachers can help in many ways. If parents have difficulty in teaching good study habits, they may be able to find a retired school teacher from the ward or stake who could be brought in to give Johnny or Mary private tutoring. A dedicated home teacher, with parental approval, might also take Johnny to his home or place of work and teach him skills he cannot learn in his own home. Mary can be taught ironing, baby care, and other home arts.

As has been seen, pre-adolescence is a very crucial period in Johnny's development. It is a stage during which he needs to measure himself against others to build his own good feelings about himself. It is another *doing* stage where skills of all kinds need to be learned. Symptoms of youth are often mistaken for impertinence. Parents need to change their methods of handling. It is a cross-roads leading either to active, happy, well-adjusted teen years, or to frustration, failure, school drop-out, and possible delinquency. Now is when intensive effort saves the most souls. The teenage years, just around the corner, are far more difficult to reprogram.

All those who help to see that Johnny, his sister Mary, and their friends are being firmly but lovingly guided through this period, sow for a rich harvest. Effective handling during these crucial years makes the teen years less turbulent and adulthood more fruitful.

Chapter 8

Adolescence

Adulthood Unrecognized

Chapter 8

Adulthood Unrecognized

Crash! Johnny is now John. He is a teenager. Adults around him begin to tread softly, hoping not to upset his delicate balance between rational and seemingly irrational behavior. Parents and other adults, expecting trouble, tend to look for the origin of the problems at this stage, but they look in vain. John is what he is. His first twelve years of life have already largely determined what kind of teenager and adult he will be. Those habits and thoughts learned from eight to twelve are far more significant in explaining behavior than those acquired in teenage years. John is already programmed. If John has problems, the challenge is to reprogram—if parents can and if John is willing. John himself may want to take some responsibility for this. Whatever his programming, he needs consistant love and respect as he embarks on this phase of life's journey.

Almost all teenagers are still struggling with the unresolved problems of earlier years. For this reason, their behavior resembles that of younger children in many ways. For many young people, especially boys, the unruly stage just described does not end at twelve but continues on to fourteen or older.

As the same time, there are special growing-up tasks and special problems associated with this, as with every phase of life. If the early programming was done skillfully in obedience to gospel principles, and if parents love and respect their children and know how to guide them while still respecting their free agency, the special tasks and problems of adolescence will be negotiated without too much anxiety.

One problem mentioned most often as characteristic of the teenager is achieving a sense of identity and personal integrity. Often there is no useful, productive role for them in society so they are kept in school long years after they feel grown up and ready to assume adult responsibilities. They have been described as "consumers, dependents, and bored observers of the adult rat race." Some become rebellious, defiant, and destructive. Drugs and illicit sex take their toll. The fault lies partly with society, partly with the young person himself, and partly with lack of strong family life and proper programming.

John has been observing and analyzing adult behavior for years. He and his sister Mary have observed the behavior of adults, and they have passed judgment. If they have grown strong through warm, understanding relationships, they are prone to emulate their parents or other adults and accept their way of life. If their judgment is negative, they tend to reject adults and all they represent.

Rejection is unfortunate for two reasons. The first is that youthful judgments are often made without much experience. Most young people are idealistic without the tempering benefits of experience. Young John rejects the adult world before he really understands the problems involved and why adults behave as they do.

The second reason why rejection is unfortunate is that John has no satisfactory alternative. He may condemn the entire society, as many youths are doing today; but what else is there? The hippy culture has already been exposed as a fraud. The extremists who react violently are totally destructive. If the adults' way won't work, what will? Those who want to tear down have nothing constructive to offer as an alternative. Hence many young people today are drifting, seeking a stable group of which they can feel a valued part. For personal integrity or self-esteem any person needs a feeling of *belonging* and of being respected and valued for himself. If the family fails and the society fails, to what will they turn? Groups of young people band together into a kind of sub-culture focusing on rock music, love, peace, and "doing their thing." The appeal is that anyone, regardless of problems, is welcomed and accepted. Each feels that he "belongs." Doing their thing is a bid for recognition as unique individuals. These groups, however, lack basic order and stability, so they offer no permanent solutions.

Latter-day Saint youth need never suffer this kind of identity crisis. There is a valued place for each one within the structure of the Church. They *know* who they are, where they came from, what they should be accomplishing on this earth, and where they are going when they leave here. They are also aware of important events which are to happen in the not-too-far-distant future. Each one can know that he was sent here to do a job and that the Lord expects him to do it regardless of what happens. Each has a significant part to play in the world drama that is unfolding. Nothing should be permitted to interfere with this. The opposition is so strong as to be almost overwhelming, but Latter-day Saints have a source of hidden power—the Holy Ghost and the gospel truths.

Young people of the Church have a great heritage, but they have an even greater future. These are they who will be participating in the great events leading to the second coming of Christ. As the polarity widens between those who will be destroyed at his coming and those who will be caught up to meet Him, young people will have to decide on which side they want to be numbered. Either they must choose to be strong and live gospel principles in harmony and unity with others, or they can choose to be destroyed.

Young people who indulge in drugs, illicit sex, violence, crime, or rebelliousness should know that they are rebelling not only against their parents and society, they are also rebelling against God. The war between Lucifer and Jesus Christ has never ended. Fortunately, Latter-day Saint youths know that they overcame Satan once in the spirit world. *They can do it again*, if they so desire. For this, however, they will have to be willing to fight. Those who drift with the tide, unconcerned regarding the future, are not likely to survive the pressures of the last days. Parents who make sure their children know these things and inspire them to be loyal to their Savior need have no fear. For them there is no identity crisis.

One pertinent question for Latter-day Saint youth is: "To what extent can I participate in business, politics, the arts, and other worldly endeavors and still accomplish all the Lord sent me down here to do?"

Much is made of the scripture that the Saints are to be "in the world but not of it." Another even more significant scripture states: "Ye are the salt of the earth: but if the salt have lost his savour, wherewith shall it be salted? It is henceforth good for nothing, but to be cast out, and to be trodden under foot of men." (Matt. 5:13.) This means that Latter-day Saints in all the world can have an influence for good wherever they are, but if they fail to be true to the laws of God and fail to stay close to him, their good influence will be lost like salt that has no flavor. Perhaps never before have Latter-day Saints had so many great opportunities to use their leadership training in constructive and stabilizing ways for the good of their fellowmen.

After an LDS youth conference in Las Vegas, Nevada, the following appeared on the front page of one of the local papers:

Gleaming faces and no dependence on drugs, cigarettes, or other stimulants denotes a quality of optimism which speaks well for the future of the community and the nation.

Conflicting views were expressed calmly and logically without confrontation and violence. That's the way youth must go to get their message across. Even the greatest truth can be obscured by unacceptable behavior. So the things the young people said and did at the Latter-day Saint gathering were impressive and in sharp focus.

Our message to those youngsters who don't like the world in which they live and want to change it is to emulate the formula and conduct of this youth gathering."[1]

This is a striking example of how youth who are strong in the gospel are making an impace in their communities

The professional literature describes the teen years as characterized by turmoil, turbulence, stress, and storm. They need not be that way. In some primitive cultures there is little or no rebelliousness among the youth because they are accepted as adults at an early age. Certain "rites of passage"—adult tasks—are required to be performed, after which the boy is officially a man. The dividing line is clear and acceptable to all.

In "civilized" cultures the change-over from childhood to adulthood takes ten years or longer. During this time the young people are in limbo. Parents treat them as children. They try to act like adults. Hence a constant tug-of-war.

For Latter-day Saint youth there are many important aids to peaceful adolescence. The frustrations of this period can be cushioned by parents who understand gospel principles and have learned how to apply them. How capable John is and how ready for independence will depend on the quality of earlier programming. What should he have learned, and how do the basic gospel principles apply during teen years?

Eternal progression: John completes his physical growth during these years, shooting up first into a gangling, awkward boy, then gradually filling out into the stature of the

---

[1]Hank Greenspun, *Las Vegas Sun*, August 1, 1970.

man he is becoming. Since the body he has is basically the one with which he will live throughout all eternity, to feel good about it is vital. If there is any defect or imperfection, real or imagined, John will suffer torments. He *must* feel acceptable to himself and to his friends. Such nicknames as "fatso," "skinny," "shrimp," or "runt" are cruel because they ridicule and call attention to his imperfections. They tear down self-respect. Parents often thoughtlessly make fun of their children in inexcusable ways just to bolster their own feelings of superiority.

Few mortals really comprehend the enormous, eternal value of the physical body. It is taken for granted. Yet scientists stand in awe of its marvelous complexity. Satan rages in despair because he will never have one. He gains a malevolent satisfaction out of persuading people to abuse or even destroy their bodies or those of others. If a person cannot control his own physical appetites and passions he becomes vulnerable to the influence of Satan, who watches ceaselessly for opportunities to take over. Some young people, for example, wonder at the strictly modest dress standards advocated by the Church. Not to observe them, however, is an open invitation to the evil one.

With physical growth comes sexual maturity and adult emotions which John and Mary struggle to understand. Assuming that the biological changes relating to puberty have already been taught, sex education in the early teen years can consist of helping them understand and evaluate in more mature ways the mass of confusing information coming to them from their culture. This should be done in terms of the insights provided by the gospel of Jesus Christ. The world does not understand the necessity for the strict moral code advocated in the Bible. To many this is a medieval superstition not worthy of serious consideration. It has been discarded without anything having been substituted. Hence, many young people are completely at sea, searching for something, they know not what. "If there is no right or wrong you might as well do what you want," stated one sixteen-year-old who was already pregnant out of wedlock.

For any youth raised in a religious home, and especially for Latter-day Saints, this constitutes a grave conflict. Two normal characteristics of the teen years create a powerful pull away from the teachings and values of adults. The first of these is the cohesiveness of the peer group. In the pre-adolescent years it was noted that John was strongly attracted to other boys, Mary to other girls. This need to be with friends becomes even stronger in the early teen years and includes both sexes. In their eagerness to grow up and become independent from parents, they lean upon their friends for emotional support. To be like them and to gain their approval is extremely important, and some people never get over it.

If John and Mary can feel accepted and comfortable with the group of young people in their ward, they will have a good chance of remaining true to the gospel principles. If they feel rejected or unappreciated by the group, they will turn to others and want to be like them. A very serious problem arises when a group of young people in a ward becomes so cliquish that they will not accept with friendliness any newcomers. Converts to the Church often have trouble being accepted if they dress or act differently, as some of them do.

Whether or not John and Mary stay with the Church group will also be influenced strongly by how they are being treated at home. If they are rebellious because parents don't respect their need to grow up, if they are still being treated like four year olds, they are likely to rebel not only against parents but against everything the parents consider important. On the other hand, if the pre-adolescent stage was handled skillfully, if they are growing in wisdom and confidence, knowing that their parents respect them and will give them as much freedom as they can handle responsibly, there will be no need for rebellion.

The second characteristic of the teen years that challenges young people about Church doctrine is the need to question and to find out for themselves about important life values. This may come during the middle or later teen years. Whether or not John or Mary remain virgins, for example, may depend upon whether they have gained a *personal* testimony of the gospel. As has been explained, when children are young they accept on faith most of what they are told. As they approach adulthood and are confronted with conflicting value systems, they want to find out for themselves what is right and true.

How parents react to this is crucial. When John asks questions about other churches, these need to be answered truthfully and fairly. What is there to fear? For parents to become panicky and start forcing religion on John is the surest method of driving him away. Free agency *must* be respected in this matter. Parents cannot force their children into heaven. That was Satan's plan.

Many Latter-day Saint parents obey the scriptures telling them that they are responsible for teaching gospel principles to their children. This is as it should be. To become over-concerned and over-protective, however, is a sure way to cause rebellion. Remember that a parent's task is to help his children grow up into strong, confident adults who are capable of thinking and acting for themselves. To do otherwise is to ignore and to try to thwart their eternal progression. John cannot learn to take the responsibility for his own life and destiny if mother and dad are constantly hovering over him, doing his thinking and making his decisions for him.

The best way to teach John and Mary to observe high moral and ethical standards is to teach them the truths of the gospel so that they know why a moral code is necessary. Then when they question, discuss with them the pros and cons, listening to their ideas and respecting their right to their own opinions. *Respect* and *human dignity* are the key words to successful association with young people.

John's growth and development during the teen years also includes preparation for his vocation or profession. Long years of schooling are required because of the vast amount of knowledge to be learned and the high quality of performance to be learned and the high quality of performance expected. Learning, of course, is one aspect of growth and needs to be continued throughout life. A school, however, is an artificial environment which may prevent a young person from assuming responsibility in society unless he can work part time or be otherwise involved.

Is it proper or wise to keep the teenager away from responsibility so long? It is one thing always to be seeking knowledge. It is quite another endlessly to defer responsibility. For one answer, look at the Lord's way. How old was Jesus when he first taught in the temple? What age was Mormon when he was general of all the Nephite armies? When did Joseph Smith receive his first vision? And at what age did President Joseph F. Smith go to Hawaii on a mission? The oldest of these was fifteen. Admittedly, these were unique individuals living in different cultures, but they represent real examples.

To say that it is not fair to young people to be kept apart from the mainstream of life does not solve the problem of how they can participate. Unless the present system undergoes a basic change, youth will continue to be restless and to feel frustrated because their eternal progression is being advanced in only one way—intellectually. They need also to be making progress along other lines. The greatest error in this, however, is the inference that they are still children, not capable of functioning as adults. This is why young people are so eager to obtain a drivers license, to own a car, to get married young, to drop out of school and get a job. They are saying, "See? I *am too* an adult."

Parents can help John and Mary by giving them responsibility at home and by helping them to feel that they are capable of functioning as adults. Although they may complain, learning to work and to enjoy achievement is essential to mental health. Here the culture again confuses the issue.

Formerly, work involved a strong back and sweat, but today it normally involves learning a process, running a machine, reading many books, and producing much paper work. This makes "work" difficult to define and this makes it hard for John to have the great experience of accomplishment through work.

Too many people consider the scriptural admonition, "In the sweat of thy face shalt thou eat bread," a tragedy, when in reality it is a blessing. The key words given two verses previous are often overlooked: "Cursed is the ground *for thy sake*." (See Genesis 3:17-19.) One of the greatest frauds today is that the work week must be reduced and that people, young and old, must have more leisure time. Apart from the morality of it, the emotional effect is devasting. Few people can maintain a healthy frame of mind when they have too much leisure time. Soon they turn inward and worry about themselves, beginning to imagine or overemphasize ailments, grievances, and fears, or seeking substitute satisfaction through physical gratification, liquor, gambling, and other destructive indulgences. People need the growth producing benefits of work to maintain social and emotional balance.

The lives of John and Mary may be so filled with activities that they literally do not have time to do much at home. Work responsibility can be learned other places, however. In school politics, club leadership, serving on committees, and doing volunteer work young people can get involved.

One of the great opportunities to assume adult responsibility comes when a young man or woman goes on a mission. The work is hard, often accomplished under adverse circumstances. It requires growth on all fronts. John must be able to discipline himself, get along with other people, and stay close to the Lord. Some go out pitifully unprepared to function as an adult. If they succeed, though, they come back mature men and women.

In viewing the responsibilities given to children in the home, a balance needs to be achieved. Sometimes, to look at the total life picture and the demands being made on each member of the family will help to decide what is important and what can be eliminated. Sometimes too much is expected too soon. A case in point is that of Mike T., age seventeen.

Mike was arrested by juvenile authorities for using foul language in a busy department store. He was the oldest of three children and the only boy. His father and mother, originally very active in the Church, were divorced when Mike was two years old, but continued to see each other occasionally. Over the years Mike's mother had grown to depend on him as though he were the father in the home. He disciplined his sisters, was consulted on financial matters, and would even sleep in his mother's bed when she was frightened.

As Mike grew into his adolescent years he was caught in a tug-of-war between his family responsibilities, especially his mother's emotional dependence on him, and his normal teenage inclinations. He performed his own tasks well, such as studying, working after school, and carrying out his priest's duties, but when his mother demanded that he act, in many ways, like a husband, he broke down. This conflict became so severe that he began to live in an unreal fantasy world where he imagined many strange adventures. He also began to hear voices. Soon, his schoolmates in their small Southern Colorado farming town began to laugh and tease him. This caused him to withdraw further until he was seldom seen outside the house.

His mother, seeing his strange behavior, began to treat him less like a man and more like a child, which frightened and confused him. Then, as she attempted to withdraw his privileges he became angry and violent. Shortly thereafter he made a scene in a department store while on a trip to Denver and was arrested and referred to his bishop. The bishop arranged for a professional evaluation in Salt Lake City.

This entire family was deeply disturbed and had been for generations. Mike's grandparents were all involved in the Church but had a distorted idea of discipline. His father had been raised under very harsh rules which had literally broken his spirit. Mike's mother, though active, was not emotionally strong enough to fight life alone and had turned to Mike for comfort and support. This had confused his programming in nearly every way. The pressure of being the man of the family finally caused him to choose the unreal but endurable world of dreams and voices rather than the real but painful world of bills, discipline, and his mother—especially his mother.

Mike's illness was so severe that it required active involvement of the therapist for several months. Eventually Mike was helped to realize among other things that he was not the head of the family. This knowledge lifted a great burden, and he returned home.

The bishop, in the meantime, had been helping Mike's mother learn how to carry the family leadership. Through the Relief Society she learned homemaking skills, budgeting, and spiritual values. Through appropriate help she was able to obtain a less time-consuming job, reduce her debts, and become financially self supporting. Through the MIA, Mike's two sisters learned about their responsibilities, both as children and as young ladies, so that they could share the family load. Finally, the bishop assigned mature home teachers who became the men in this family's life. He was careful to warn them to keep an appropriate emotional and physical distance between them and Mike's mother, for she was naturally very lonely.

Mike progressed very well after he was relieved of his pressure-filled role. He is not married yet because he is still recovering from his "first marriage." Nevertheless, he is well on the way to a full, mentally healthy life.

This is one example of reprogramming or correcting the faulty ideas with which a boy had been struggling for years. His eternal progression was being warped by the unrealistic demands made upon him.

Another key factor in adolescent development is faith. In chapter one it was noted that small babies need to be learning trust in others as a basic foundation for faith in themselves. At three Johnny learned to be obedient without losing his good feelings about himself. He was taught about God. At six, faith in himself, or self-respect, marked the beginnings of masculinity. It also gave him confidence. Johnny had faith in himself, but his parents found it hard to trust him because they failed to recognize his abilities and the fact that he was on the threshold of adolescence.

Teenagers need faith in themselves and their ability to find a place in the adult world. Even those who reject the adult culture carefully copy any aspect of it that helps them feel grown up and important. Drinking, drugs, and sex fall in this category. The decisions teenagers face will be strongly influenced by their integrity or lack of it. Will they be true to what they believe to be correct principles? Do they know correct principles? Do they have a personal philosophy of life?

Knowing correct principles is not enough, though. John needs to make decisions based on self-respect. If he has too much self-respect to swear or cheat or take drugs, he wears a suit of moral armor. This self-respect grows as his parents respect him. They literally teach him respect as they speak, act, and demonstrate respect.

The issue of long hair, for example, assumes it's proper perspective. Long hair is not a question of immorality. It is basically a question of John's wearing a hair style that fits his self-image. Scraggly, dirty hair often mirrors John's inner self. Certainly shoulder-length hair is disconcerting on a boy. On the other hand, if John is clean, neat, and takes responsibility, why argue? Eventually enough adults will probably adopt these fads so that John will get a crewcut to be different.

In issues like hair, skirt lengths, and other fads, adults tend to focus on the symptoms rather than the basic problem. The symptom is the current fad, while the basic factor is the individual's integrity or lack of it.

To test this, it is interesting to challenge a teenage girl on her moral standards. Joan P., age thirteen, came in after referral by her parents, who stated her to be immoral and incorrigible. Their specific complaint focused on her skirts. Even if she had left home with a knee-length skirt she would pull up the top at school and walk around with her garters exposed. Her worried parents thought she was intentionally exposing her body to the boys and spent many hours preaching to her on the subject of morals. This was like saying, "We don't like you the way you are." It was an attack on her integrity as a person. It tore down her faith in herself.

Joan, as the interviewer saw her, was an exceptionally bright, very pretty thirteen-year-old. Her skirt was truly mini, and because she was so attractive, the effect portrayed her to be much older. Nevertheless, emotionally she was still thirteen years old, and her major hope was to be part of her group, rather than seducing every boy in sight, as her parents feared she was doing. To test this, the interviewer resorted to rather blunt tactics. He invited her to put her feet upon the desk and be comfortable. Her face turned bright scarlet, and she was offended. He then asked her why she was embarrassed; her skirt was so short it didn't hide much anyway. This remark hit home, and though perhaps rough, it convinced him that Joan was not the seductress her parents thought her to be. It also affected Joan's thinking.

They next discussed why the styles of her friends were so important that Joan would defy her parents, Church leaders, and school teachers. The fact was that Joan and her parents seldom talked in a conversational way. The parents often preached at her, but never let her speak freely of her hopes, problems, and other personal ideas. They literally did not know her. They had no faith in her so consequently she turned to her friends with whom she could relax and find security. Her friends wore miniskirts; hence, to be comfortable with them she wore mini-skirts. This had very little to do with her sexual-moral standards. It had a great deal to do with her normal needs for friends, attention, and acceptance. Her faith in herself was a mirror of how her friends felt about her. If she was popular, her self-image was great. If not, it took a nose dive. Everyone, especially teenagers, needs to feel good about himself, to have faith in himself as a human being. What was the solution? Joan's parents had to re-evaluate their time schedule, their disciplinary methods, and their own priorities. They were basically fine people, but they had seriously neglected some fundamental rules of family life. To correct matters, first they began to have family home evenings. With each member participating, after several months they had relaxed enough to begin communicating. It was hard for Joan's father to stop lecturing her everytime he felt the need, but he worked at it. Eventually, Joan began to volunteer comments about her problems and seek advice from her parents. They listened, and many times did not make decisions but offered their opinions, leaving Joan a choice. As they respected her she began to respect herself. The family began to slip away every week or so for a picnic or a ride. At dinner time criticism or arguments were forbidden so that everyone felt "safe."

    Joan's parents did not decrease their vigilance over her, they actually increased it because she was so open now that she kept them informed. Months went by, and the skirts stayed short, but her parents did not berate her about it. As her parents' faith in her increased, her need to flaunt extreme styles decreased. The more comfortable she felt with her parents, the less dependent she became upon the approval of her friends. Faith in herself and an awareness of personal integrity gradually developed. She and her parents finally reached a solution on skirt lengths.

Often the greatest challenge to a teenagers' parents is to differentiate between healthy individuality and dangerous rebellion. Joan's parents found that once they realized her skirts were only a symptom and that the problem was actually a need for love and respect as a human being, they could begin to cope with the situation. They were not helpless, and Joan was not unwilling. She needed a reason to be cooperative, and their love and faith finally gave it to her.

The subject of *free agency* as related to young people is a touchy one. Eventually John is going to demand the use of his God-given right to choose for himself, whether he knows how to use the gift wisely or not. Because he is still lacking in good judgment, parents are reluctant to give him the freedom that he feels is his right.

Respecting free agency does not mean that parents relinquish all supervision. The way the Lord handled Adam and Eve in the garden of Eden is a good example. He—

1. Told them the rule or principle. (Of every tree of the garden thou mayest freely eat, but of the tree of knowledge of good and evil, thou shalt not eat.)
2. Told them the consequences of disobedience. (In the day that thou eatest thereof thou shalt surely die.)
3. Forbade them to break the rule. (Remember that I forbid it.)
4. But gave them their free agency. (Nevertheless, thou mayest choose for thyself, for it is given unto thee.)

This placed the responsibility upon the shoulders of Adam and Eve.

How might this be applied to an older teenager? Suppose John comes to his parents and asks permission to go to a party. The parents, upon questioning, find that there will be drinking. Using the above formula, the parents would—

1. State the principle. (Drinking is dangerous and degrading.)
2. Help him think through consequences (possibility of indulging, temporary loss of judgment and control during which anything can happen, etc.).
3. Forbid it. (Say to him: "If you are asking my permission, the answer is no.")
4. Give him his free agency. ("I know, however, that I cannot *force* you not to go, nor would I want to. The decision, therefore, is up to you. I know I can trust you to choose wisely. If, however, you choose to go to this party anyway, knowing that it is wrong and that I have forbidden it, the consequences will be yours, and you will have to live with them.")

This method accomplishes several things: (1) it gives John some information on which to base his decision; (2) by recognizing his free agency it *removes any justifiable reason for him to rebel*; (3) it places the responsibility for his conduct on his own shoulders, where it should be; and (4) it still maintains the dignity and authority of the parent.

Many parents will find this method difficult because they cannot bear to see their child, whom they love and whose success in life is important to them, deliberately choose to do wrong. No one, however, can live another person's life for him. *The chance that he will choose to do wrong is enormously greater if parents try to force him to do right.* To John, his personal integrity and right of free agency are being threatened, and these he must defend at all cost.

As indicated in chapter two, living happy, mentally healthy lives depends upon three factors: (1) a knowledge of the laws of God, (2) the will to obey, and (3) power to control. These all come into sharp focus for John during the teen years. Knowledge of the gospel has been available to him since early childhood through the lives and teachings of parents, through all Church classes and activities, and through the examples set by Church leaders and other good people. These examples will also help give John the will to obey. If he likes and admires any adult, he will want to become like that person. For this reason parents *must* respect their teenage children and leave them free to grow up. They must learn how to talk to them man-to-man or woman-to-woman, still allowing them the right to their own opinions. Teenagers cannot be treated like young children without destroying their self-respect. When this happens, the good influence of parents is nullified. If John's father or mother is still trying to make all his decisions and expecting instant obedience, John may leave home in search of someone who will listen to him and appreciate him.

The following is a letter written by such a boy. At the age of thirteen he already had a record as a juvenile delinquent.

Dear Folks,
    Thank you for everything, but I am going to Chicago and try and start some kind of a new life.

    You asked me why I did those things and why I gave you so much trouble, and the answer is easy for me to give you, but I am wondering if you will understand.

    Remember when I was about six or seven and I used to want you to just listen to me? I remember all the nice things you gave me for Christmas and my birthday and I was really happy with things—about a week—at the time I got the things, but the rest of the time during the year I really didn't want presents, I just wanted all the time for you to listen to me like I was somebody who felt things too, because I remember even when I was young I felt things. But you said you were busy.

    Mom, you are a wonderful cook, and you had everything so clean and you were tired so much from doing all those things that made you busy; but, you know something Mom? I would have liked crackers and peanut butter just as well—if you had only sat down with me a while during the day and said to me: "Tell me all about it so I can maybe help you understand."

And when Donna came I couldn't understand why everyone made so much fuss because I didn't think it was my fault that her hair is curly and her skin so white, and she doesn't have to wear glasses with such thick lenses. Her grades were better too, weren't they?

If Donna ever has children, I hope you will tell her to just pay some attention to the one that doesn't smile very much because that one will really be crying inside. And when she's about to bake six dozen cookies to make sure first that the kids don't want to tell her about a dream or a hope or something, because thoughts are important too, to small kids even though they don't have so many words to use when they tell about what they have inside them.

I think that all the kids who are doing so many things that grown-ups are tearing out their hair worrying about are really looking for somebody that will have time to listen a few minutes and really and truly will treat them as they would a grown-up who might be useful to them, you know—polite to them. If you folks had ever said to me "Pardon me" when you interrupted me, I'd have dropped dead!

If anybody asks you where I am, tell them I've gone looking for somebody with time because I've got a lot of things I want to talk about.

Love to all, Your son[2]

John's *will to obey* will also be influenced by faith in God and the ability to pray effectively. Rebellion against parents leads to rebellion against God. Faith in parents leads to faith in God, providing, of course, that father and mother are faithful and strong in the gospel. If the spirit of the Lord is felt in the home day by day and the power of the priesthood used to bless and guide the family, John will absorb this and want to obey the commandments of God so that he can become like Him.

If John gets this far, he still has one more hurdle: the *power to control*. He may want to do right but not have the moral strength to make himself do it. This ability should have been growing since he was two years old.

---

[2]Distrubuted by South Suburban Juvenile Officers' Association, Kansas City, Missouri.

Every time mother took him firmly by the hand and insisted that he do as he was told he was getting practice in doing the right thing, even when the activity did not look attractive to him. Children who are spoiled and allowed always to do what looks easy, fun, or desirable at the moment without regard for future consequences, will grow up to be moral weaklings. If John did not learn this early in life, he may be in trouble during the teen years. Parents cannot teach him in this way at this late date because they cannot demand obedience. His free agency must be respected. If he learns to control himself it will be the hard way—by making mistakes and discovering for himself that a person cannot be happy and get along with other people by being selfish and headstrong. Such a person will have trouble succeeding in school, holding a job, staying married.

Repentance is also vital for any teenager. If the use of this principle was learned earlier (see chapter 7) John will be handling most of his mistakes satisfactorily without their becoming millstones around his neck. He will cope with guilt feelings and use the mistakes as learning experiences. His confidence and sense of personal integrity will permit him to make mistakes without feeling ashamed. To learn is to grow.

If John has little faith in himself, fear of failure will prevent his experiencing life fully and deeply. If repentance is not viewed as a useful tool for dealing with life experiences, John may continue in wrongdoing, defending his actions instead of correcting them. If parents are still carrying all the responsibility for his actions by trying to make all his decisions and force him to do right, John may not see the need for repentance. His life may be tragically and unnecessarily handicapped.

The subject of *love* is also a big one for teenagers, and sometimes it is confusing. As described in chapter two, spiritual love involves intermingling of congenial spirits. It is life-giving and sustaining. While teenagers are trying to become emotionally less dependent upon their parents, the need for this kind of love is intense. It is heightened by the physical desire to be close to one of the opposite sex.

In the early teen years the physical attraction may be so intense that it becomes confused with spiritual love. Some people, even adults, never do discover the difference. Yet without spiritual, life-giving love, a person will be dissatisfied and unhappy.

Those who have grown up unable to give or receive love will drift from one lover to another, in and out of marriages, always searching but never finding happiness. The spirit suffers, being deprived and undernourished. The person cannot understand why physical love does not satisfy the deep, gnawing hunger.

John and Mary need to know about this, and that physical love without the spiritual cannot give them what they really want and need most. It is possible for a person to be relatively happy without physical love, but no one can be happy without spiritual love. People need other people.

John may think he wants to be independent, but what he really is working towards is shifting his emotional dependence from his parents to a wife. This is not an infantile dependence in which one does most of the giving and the other most of the taking, but a healthy interdependence in which the man and the woman each give freely to make the other happy and receive freely without having their autonomy threatened. To achieve this, John must be a mature, confident, unselfish person in his own right, and so must his girl. At sixteen or eighteen he is still working toward that kind of maturity and will encounter rough going if he gets married before he is ready.

Church authorities, seeing the sorrow that follows early sexual relations and early marriages, have suggested that Latter-day Saint youth wait until the age of sixteen to date.

By that age, John and Mary will be physically and emotionally ready to enjoy a closer relationship with other young people. Earlier they were too immature to handle the stresses of emotional involvements, but now they can survive the joys and sorrows of male-female togetherness.

As with every other stage of life, how John and Mary treat sex at this stage is directly related to life at home. If they are loved and respected, they will usually wait for similar treatment from their boy or girl friend. Mary will not want a premature marriage or sexual experience if she has an image of a mature male partner as learned from dad. This is her armor. John will not casually violate a girl's chastity if his father has taught him to respect women and his mother has set a worthy example.

One sad situation illustrates the importance of mature love in the home.

Debra was pregnant out of wedlock. She was also very rebellious at home. She was a bright eighteen-year-old girl, the youngest of five children. All of her brothers and sisters were much older, so she was raised as an only child. Debra had completed high school and one year at college. She was a rather attractive girl who dressed neatly and had a nice figure. She had artistic talent and was a good student. Her family was very active in the Church, but her mother was so active that nothing else seemed important, including Debra. Her father was so stern that she was afraid of him. Sometimes he cursed and swore at her when she made mistakes or misbehaved. Since her parents were middle aged when she was born, they seemed like grandparents to her. She felt that they did not understand her. She received absolutely no sex education from them as she grew up. During one summer at home Debra became involved with a young man from a rather disorganized Latter-day Saint family. He had many emotional problems. They thought they were in love, but when she became pregnant he backed away from marriage.

Debra was deeply involved emotionally, and although she realized that he was a poor marriage risk, she could not bring herself to break away from him. As the pregnancy progressed, he gave her no emotional support, until she was eventually convinced that there was no hope. She finally decided to give up the baby for adoption. After this was over she returned to her home, then to school.

Debra was an intelligent, sensitive girl who needed a great deal of love. As she grew up she was not close to either parent, nor to any of her brothers or sisters. Almost from birth she seldom experienced love and trust. Her parents were both so preoccupied during her formative years that in her teen years she blamed the Church for taking them away from her. Her mother, although not home much, was possessive and over-protective, so that Debra did not learn self-reliance. Church activity was forced on her until she developed a deep antagonism against it. She was deeply hurt by her father's harsh treatment. Art work became her main emotional outlet. When she met the father of her child, it was like opening emotional floodgates for both her and the boy, but since both were basically self-centered, this relationship, too, was doomed to failure. Debra again felt rejected and unloved. Giving up her baby was an additional deprivation, but she loved him enough to want him to have a chance in live in a good adoptive home.

Fortunately, Debra had enough confidence in her bishop to go to him when she first realized she was pregnant. Physical arrangements for her during her pregnancy took first priority. The bishop referred her to the Church adoption agency. To give her the best chance to start over, she went to live in another home in the same community. The caseworker and the bishop provided counseling and emotional support while she was working through her feelings about her parents, the Church, the father of her child, the baby, and herself. One of the most effective people, however, was a ward Relief Society sister on special assignment, who had also been a YWMIA worker for years. This good woman spent many hours listening to and loving Debra. She permitted her to question the gospel, even express bitter feelings about what the Church had allegedly done to her. Eventually, because of this sister's patience, Debra began to see her parents as people with problems of their own who did love her but had many frustrations.

She came to see herself as an intelligent person who was capable of making realistic plans for her future. Her feelings about the Church softened enough for her to regain some faith in God, but she found it difficult to believe in a *Father* in heaven because her idea of a father did not include love. At least her ideas were her own, however, and not something forced on her. She was thinking instead of just reacting emotionally.

After Debra released her baby she went home briefly, then away to attend an eastern college. Her bishop contacted the ward at the college, suggesting that she be invited and encouraged, but not pressured, into renewing her associations with the Church. Debra still had a long way to go, but at least she was facing in the right direction and had taken the first steps. Enough loving concern, through the institute of religion especially, may eventually thaw her frozen heart enough to embrace the gospel again.

This type of sadness need not occur. As has been mentioned, if love and respect are residents in the home, then children and adults will not seek immoral substitutes.

Of course, given the best of environments—if certain basic safeguards are violated—then trouble will follow. Practically speaking, there are many reasonable rules that can prevent sexual transgression. These need to be taught and followed because the finest young men and women have quite normal drives. A man's background won't save him if he voluntarily steps into quicksand.

If the priests quorum secretary dates the bishop's daughter and their homes are healthy, they are still tampering with sexual explosives if they go beyond certain limits:

1. Single dating is not always fun or safe.
2. Parking alone in lover's lane is useful for only two things—illicit sexual activity and falling prey to predatory criminals. Neither is recommended for a happy life.
3. The length of time alone together has direct bearing on sexual intimacy. One very promiscuous girl never had sexual relations until she had been with a boy for at least three hours, then she was lost *every* time.
4. Suggestive movies, conversation, literature are simply a way of lighting the fuse.
5. Certain parts of the body, if caressed, create sexual excitement that leads directly to intercourse.
6. Alcohol and drugs are expensive, one-way streets to cheap sex. One rather disturbed young woman could not recall having a sexual experience without liquor. A boy can have sexual intercourse *with any girl he wants* if he can get her to take a few drinks.
7. Parties where alcohol and drugs are used as a prelude to sex lead to many tragedies. Twelve-year-old girls have become pregnant this way.

While John and Mary are being taught about love, they also need to understand realistically that temptations such as these exist and should be avoided. Parents cannot protect their children from all evil, but they can help them think through crisis situations before they happen. For example, during some family home evening questions such as these might be discussed.

1. If your boy friend took you to a party where the kids started drinking and smoking marijuana (not knowing ahead of time that it was going to be this kind of party), what would you do?
2. If your friends see a beautiful, high powered car with the keys in the ignition and want to "borrow" it for a ride, would you go with them? What if they called you a chicken?
3. You are in love. You tke your girl home and she invites you in. Her parents are not home. How do you deal with this?

With a little imagination, parents or teachers can think of other situations in which gospel standards are being challenged. If John and Mary are permitted to talk freely and express opinions, they think out for themselves the answers to such questions. The solution, then, is *theirs*, not something forced upon them by adults. When the crisis occurs they know what to do and want to do it.

Unity in the home is a powerful deterrent to wrongdoing. If John and Mary have felt, ever since they were young children, that they were valued, respected members of the family—even when they feel the urge to stand on their own feet, or when they leave home—true affection will continue between them and other family members. They will want to merit the approval of those who love them. If home is just a place where people sleep and eat, and where sometimes even meals are irregular, John will turn elsewhere for his loyalties and his standards of conduct.

If there has never been much closeness or enjoyment of shared activities in a family, to try to achieve this when the children have become teenagers will be frustrating. For example, family home evenings need to be started when children are young and continued on into the teen years. Trying to start when the older children are already receiving major life satisfactions outside of the home will often be difficult.

To remain close to one's children and at the same time let them grow up and form loving relationships with others is quite a challenge to parents. They demonstrate their love when they think enough of a child to permit him to live his own life.

Chapter 9
Adulthood
Childhood Revisited

Chapter 9

Childhood Revisited

Now John has grown into a man. Mary has developed into a lovely young woman. The joys and satisfactions of marriage beckon. Heavy adult responsibilities lie in wait. Are they ready for these?

Adulthood is not a new life, unrelated to what has come before; it is actually an extension of childhood and adolescence. The boundary marker is marriage, in most instances, even though getting married does not change a child into an adult. If John's prior life has been healthy, he will be prepared for the experience of finding a life partner, thus taking a major step toward adulthood. This step is usually underestimated. Marriage means two separate personalities deciding to spend the rest of their lives learning to make the other person and several children happy.

As John courts and eventually marries his beloved, the passion and pleasure of their relationship make it relatively easy to get along. As they go through the ceremony of marriage, the reception, the wedding night, the emotions involved are rather unrealistic and temporary. Eventually the realities of married life set in, and John finds himself alone with his wife.

These two people face each other across the table, in bed, at church, in the myriad situations that make up life. Whether they realize it or not, they are far from the united couple they think the wedding ceremony made them. In real fact, they are still John and his wife, products of separate homes, separate schools, and separate friends. Fortunately, if they both live and love the gospel, they have something extremely powerful in common. The fact remains, though, that these two partners were very recently adolescents, and the task of becoming united has just begun. In essence, two people, still influenced by the immaturities of childhood, have married each other.

All the traits, all the lessons, all the programming that have occurred separately do not culminate now in a unity of matrimonial bliss but may actually cause problems. This is one of the delusions by which our romantic culture handicaps people. It is true that John and his wife have moved closer in their separate orbits, attracted by various influences, one of which is sexual (all too often the predominant influence). Even with these attractions, their emotional orbits are separate. More precisely, their programming takes into account very little of the other person's world. Thus, unless specific steps are taken, their orbits will remain separate. This means that these two individuals will remain individuals until they reprogram their brains to take the other into full account.

As an example, for several years John has been choosing the movies he attends. During the courtship, he probably took his girl's interest into account. This is normal. Once having secured her partnership, however, the real test of his programming comes. Does he continue to think of her interests, or does he slip back to serving his own interests? How many saintly women have endured years of attending western movies with husbands who have never remotely considered the type of film that could interest their spouses?

Which movies a couple sees is a minor problem, but the principle involved is perhaps the key to happy marital life. Partners in *successful* marriages spend more time thinking about their spouse's needs than they do their own. It is not even fifty-fifty. The point is that John is the product of many years of single living. He must consciously open his brain and permit reprogramming so that he truly becomes part of a team instead of just John. He must think and act in terms of two people, not one. The same is true, of course, of his wife.

The underlying principle is what Jesus was talking about when he said "My father and I are one." They are two separate, distinct beings, each with his own forceful, dynamic personality. Yet they work together in such unity and harmony that it is as though they were one. So must it be with John and his wife if they expect to achieve celestial bliss. They have a lifetime in which to achieve this, but the sooner they learn the happier they will be.

In all marriages, however, problems will arise and adjustments will have to be made. In endeavoring to solve these, each must understand himself and his spouse as individuals so that together they can begin to see how they are affecting each other. To focus on one person only, or each separately, is not enough. The interaction between them must be understood. Surface irritations are symptoms of unmet needs, and to solve the problem they need to delve deeper in search of basic causes.

This is one of the chief factors in analyzing a marriage. Too often the symptoms are so obvious that the real, underlying ailment is missed. For example, Brother and Sister L. were very active in the Church. They had sufficient money and status. Both came from active Latter-day Saint families. Yet, they were so dissatisfied that they were contemplating divorce. Initially, the bishop saw the problem as a mystery and could not understand why they would give up so much so easily. He wondered if another woman was involved, or if some hidden sin was preying on Sister L.'s mind. Then, using the concept of childhood programming, he began analyzing them as children. He found that Brother L. had been spoiled as a child by parents who gave him almost anything material that he sought. They did not give him their time and affection, though, so he was literally programmed to get satisfaction from things, not people. His wife's childhood was the opposite. Her parents were almost proud of their poverty. She had therefore developed a contempt for material things. This caused her to be as blind to Brother L.'s accomplishments as he was to her needs. He worked hard to provide a nice home and all the latest gadgets and appurtenances. She, who would have been happy in a humble home, found the care of all these rich trappings a burden. The total relationship was much more complex, but this was one of the basic problems. In this sense, these two physical adults were emotional children.

The bishop pointed this out to them and allowed them to think and talk about it, then he gave them Church assignments that would help them work on their problem. He also met with them about once a month for six months to help them evaluate their progress. He did not permit them to beat around the bush, but discussed their problems frankly with them. The key to success was not so much what the bishop did but how he viewed their problem. Once he saw them for the children they were, other pieces fell into place.

Finances is always an area of real concern. It takes time and is a trial to find the balance between needs and wishes. Couples often disagree on what is essential and what is a luxury. The breaking point comes when one person becomes intolerant of the other. One such couple were Brother and Sister J. Both were college graduates, both had served missions, and both came from active Latter-day Saint families in the same ward. On the surface their backgrounds seemed ideal, especially concerning money, since both families were frugal. Finances soon became an issue, however, as Brother J. began to behave in a manner that made Scrooge look like a spendthrift. He objected to spending money on new clothes, food, entertainment, and other expenses that most people consider essential.

This couple went to their bishop, or rather Sister J. fled in tears to her bishop. Wisely he looked beyond the surface picture of two so-called adults engaged in a silly dispute. He took the time to find out about Brother J.'s early years when his father was struggling to get started. Brother J. had memories of his worried father trying to make each paycheck stretch. He also found that Brother J., though a man of many abilities, lacked self-confidence and felt more secure with a large bank balance. With Sister J. he noted that she, as an only daughter, had been rather indulged, especially in buying clothes.

In a very common breakdown of marital communications the J.'s had not discussed any of these problems with each other. Under the firm guidance of the bishop they made some concrete decisions about solving these issues. One step was to agree on a bank balance that would relieve Brother J's tension. Sister J. was given an allowance that she was permitted to spend any way she wanted, no strings attached. In their interviews the bishop had to be rather specific sometimes, such as pointing out to Brother J. that milk was important.

It would be stretching the point to say they lived happily ever after. This is seldom the case. It was very true, however, that the J.'s began to relax as each learned what made the other happier. As each learned to communicate his needs and was understood by the other, dividends accrued. The marriage reversed its downward trend to an upward spiral of love and respect. Eventually (two years later) they had developed habits of peace and communication that made them expect harmony—a new experience.

It took work and involved ups and downs, but in time they were well on their way toward a congenial relationship.

The unity between a husband and wife can be strengthened or weakened by in-laws. For John to be greatly influenced by his parents, whether or not the situation at home was pleasant, is only natural. When he marries, there is no button to push that cuts off his feelings about them. They, too, still love their son. Ideally, parents will realize that a young couple must develop their own pattern of living and leave them free to do this.

There is also the matter of priesthood authority. In the patriarchal order a man stands at the head of his family and has authority over them. When a daughter marries a man who holds the priesthood, her father relinquishes direct authority over her to her hsuband. When a son marries, he assumes the priesthood authority for his wife and the children who will come into his home. His father can still administer the affairs of the larger family, for example calling all the children and grandchildren together for a family reunion. He is not, however, directly responsible for what goes on in the homes of his married sons and daughters. This is similar to the stake president as related to a bishop. He administers the affairs of the stake as a whole and is available for consultation when needed. He also meets with the bishops regularly to discuss mutual problems. He does not, however, tell the bishop how to run his ward.

In a family situation these principles still hold true, but in modern America the larger, extended family is not expected to function as an organized unit. The patriarchal order nevertheless is the government by which God rules and orders the universe. The family is the basic unit.

> It sometimes happens that the Elders are called in to administer to the members of a family. Among these Elders there may be Presidents of Stakes, Apostles, or even members of the First Presidency of the Church. It is not proper under these circumstances for

the father to stand back and expect the Elders to direct the administration of this important ordinance. The father is there. It is his right and it is his duty to preside. (If the father be absent, the mother should request the presiding authority present to take charge.) The father presides at the table, at prayer, and gives general directions relating to his family life whoever may be present. Wives and children should be taught to feel that the patriarchal order in the Kingdom of God has been established for a wise and beneficent purpose, and should sustain the head of the household and encourage him in the discharge of his duties, and do all in their power to aid him in the exercise of the rights and privileges which God has bestowed upon the head of the home. This patriarchal order has its divine spirit and purpose, and those who disregard it under one pretext or another are out of harmony with the spirit of God's laws as they are ordained for recognition in the home. It is not merely a question of who is perhaps the best qualified. Neither is it wholly a question of who is living the most worthy life. It is a question largely of law and order, and its importance is seen often from the fact that the authority remains and is respected long after a man is really unworthy to exercise it.[1]

This quotation makes clear the necessity for John to assume his responsibilities as head of his family and for his wife and parents to respect, support, and encourage him in this position. Even if the President of the Church should walk into his home, John would still be the patriarchal authority and would take charge of the situation.

Most of the problems between married children and their parents stem from the failure of parents to relinquish authority and from a husband or wife who lets them do this instead of shouldering his own responsibilities. Part of a parent's duty is to raise his children in such a way that they will be prepared for this. Many young people marry in the temple, thus entering into the vast eternal patriarchal order, with little understanding of the solemnity of the occasion and the high order of life into which they are entering. Tension and conflict lie in wait for the married couple who do not effectively grow away from too much involvement with father and mother. Parents who

---
[1] John A. Widtsoe, *Priesthood and Church Government* (Salt Lake City: Deseret Book Co., 1954), pp. 82-83.

permit or encourage such ties are crippling their child's marriage.

They should take direction from the Lord here. He said:

> Therefore shall a man leave his father and his mother, and shall cleave unto his wife: and they shall be one flesh. (Gen. 2:24.)

Lingering, unhealthy parental involvement after marriage has caused much trouble for many fine young couples who are struggling with the ordinary adjustments of a beginning marriage.

Specifically, in-law trouble comes from three unhealthy situations. One is that so long as John's time and energies are demanded by his parents, the wife and children may be neglected. They are sure to resent this. Another is that many decisions are made in the first days, weeks, and months of marriage that need to be made as partners without third party involvement. If the partners are relatively free from distraction, they tend to work out life-long solutions. If they are trying to please both their parents and spouse then life-long problems can result. The two newly-weds are especially sensitive, too, so that wounds hurt more and remain open longer. A third problem is the temptation to go home to mother when the situation becomes difficult, instead of working together on the solution to problems. Many young couples marry without having learned to master their frustrations, irritations, and anger. Some never do. In chapter 5 a quotation from Ephesians explained that it is no sin to become angry, but it is a sin to stay that way so that Satan can enter in, intensify the feelings, and confuse the issues. Biting words expressed in anger cut deep and are hard to forgive. An angry person is not thinking clearly, and so cannot solve problems wisely. A husband and wife who, after a cooling-off period, can sit down and talk out a problem, trying to understand, listening and respecting each other's ideas, are on their way toward the warm, congenial relationship each desires. "Let not the sun go down upon your wrath" is still good advice.

As with childhood, a marriage with a strong foundation can survive many stresses. This sounds reasonable, but what far too many couples assume is that happiness will come automatically, especially if the couple were sealed in the temple and are active in the Church.

Brother and Sister M. felt this way, but after twelve years and five children they were contemplating divorce. They were married in the temple; he was a returned missionary, she a devoted mother. Each had given long hours to Church service. Yet, they were in the bishop's office saying that divorce seemed to be the only solution.

The facts of the case were interesting. Brother M. was a professional man whose father was a plumber. He was deeply involved with his father to the point where he had always consulted with him about everything—even whether or not to have more children—and blindly followed advice. From early childhood he had been very dependent on his father. Brother M. was a capable Church worker who had served in a bishopric and was high priests group leader. His wife was an extremely able teacher of youth in the MIA and was often called upon to speak to the youth. As they devoted their time and energies to the Church, they ignored the many frictions that arose between them. He was somewhat loose with money, while she worried over every penny. She clashed with his parents. He was far too busy to do things with the children. They seldom had home evenings. Family prayers were rare occasions. Family outings were few and tense and were usually cut short by expressions of ill feelings.

The M.'s "got away" with this for years until their oldest child, a sensitive twelve-year-old, began to rebel. The child disliked Church, fought with her parents, and generally raised havoc. The M.'s were deeply disturbed because they felt they had done what was expected of them and therefore their **children** should grow up properly.

As they discussed their affairs with the bishop they began to see that they had invested very little in their family unit. In some ways their only investment was to provide bodies for five spirits and a roof for their protection. They came to realize that their list of priorities was mixed up. Sister M. put all those MIA children ahead of her own offspring. She would have hobbled to an MIA meeting on crutches but often brushed off her daughter's questions at home. Brother M. would gnash his teeth when the high priests failed to have one hundred percent home teaching, but his activity with his boys was about ten percent.

This pattern of misplaced priorities was repeated in almost everything the M.'s did at home. They were not evil people, nor were they intentionally neglectful. They were laboring under a serious delusion, though, as they left the well-being of their family to chance.

The solution to their problem was quite simple, but not easy. Amidst all their worthwhile activities they had failed to build a marriage. Their present need was to remedy this lack. Specifically, Brother M. began to limit contacts with his father to areas unrelated to his family. He did consider and respect his father's opinions but reserved the right to think for himself and to make decisions with his wife for the good of the family. He began to hold home evening and family prayer. He was not particularly comfortable at planning family outings so Sister M. conducted while he presided. Sister M. began including her daughter in her MIA work. She asked for her opinion on lessons and talks. Not surprisingly, she gained valuable insights from her daughter and came to feel the pulse of youth better. In several family councils, children and parents all discussed how to improve family relations. Many important things were said, although conversation was strained at first.

What the parents heard was not always pleasant or easy for them to accept. Their natural inclination wavered between anger and hurt as the children spoke with the candor only children have. Then, as the children acquired a sense of power, they tended to be impertinent, almost disrespectful. It seemed to the M.'s that the children were going to take over. A truth about children, though, is that they do not want too much freedom too early. Children are usually *driven* into total breaks from their parents by the pressures at home; they seldom voluntarily choose complete separation. Eventually balance was restored. A sweet spirit of love and cooperation replaced the old feelings of tension. The M.'s found that as they worked hard to improve their family, their Church work improved measurably. Brother M. found that he could enjoy his father far more in his new, more mature, role. As man and woman the M.'s rediscovered each other. All this was made possible by their willingness, plus regular check-ups with the bishop, who very pointedly helped them keep their eyes on the goals.

One basic principle here was communication, which may well be the factor upon which every marriage grows or fails. Endless stories of suffering and frustration are told to bishops and marriage counselors about the lack of communication within marriages. There is a stereotype of the man who regularly comes home, reads the paper, then watches television until he goes to bed. This is repeated nearly every day, and he cannot understand why his wife is upset. A man does need rest and relaxation, but not to the exclusion of his family.

Sometimes the husband or the wife is a very quiet person who is afraid to express opinions for fear of arousing anger or ridicule. The other spouse must then be very understanding and patient, being willing to listen and drawing out his mate's ideas in an atmosphere that is calm and safe. Many problems occur within marriages simply because one or the other will not tell his mate what is bothering him. To "suffer in silence" is not a virtue in a situation such as this. These people need to take the time and make the effort to learn to share their ideas, their feelings, their hurts, but not in anger.

Even in serious areas such as finances, child raising, religion, sex, or any other crucial matters, married people often fail to communicate reasonably. Brother and Sister W. had been married twenty-two years, but she never knew his favorite food or his pet peeve. He had no notion of her skills or hobbies. Nevertheless, they had managed to bear seven children, and to some people that meant that the W.'s had a good marriage. What they did not realize was that Sister W., a very bright woman, had not enjoyed the pleasure of a conversation with her husband since he had proposed. It would have been humorous, except that she was a desperate woman.

Speech is not the only form of communication, especially in marriage. One unpolished, quiet husband awakened his wife most mornings by placing a freshly picked flower on her pillow. She did not need to hear words to know he cared. Some partners take walks, others share hobbies, many read to each other. There are as many ways to communicate as there are ideas, and no one has much of a defense by saying, "We don't know what to do." In fact, what really happens is that priorities become confused so that people fail to put any energy into their relationship; thus it gradually dwindles to nothing.

Scheduling sometimes helps. Many couples plan on one night per week when they date each other without the children or other adults being present. Some slippery husbands say they cannot afford this much high life, even though they probably went out every night while they were courting. Be that as it may, any man can walk or ride with his wife, or sit in the back yard holding her hand. There are no excuses. Some men think of a date only in terms of sex, rather than as an opportunity to talk and explore minds and feelings. These men literally do not know their wives. Precious opportunities are lost.

Too many people worry about the letter of the law

concerning communication. One brother, who was faced with the break-up of his third marriage called the counselor, frantically seeking the "right" words to say to his aggravated mate. The bishop—more in exasperation than inspiration—suggested that Brother X. just tell her he was a louse but he loved her, and then show it. Nothing was heard for days, until Brother X. left a message saying, "Tell the bishop it works." His wife was starved for genuine affection and honesty, not for fancy words.

Prayer together is good communication, but many couples cannot achieve this. Either the prayers are ritual and meaningless, or the couple does not pray at all. A husband and wife must be able to share their deep thoughts and feelings before they can pray effectively together. If the wife, for example, is very spiritual and the husband quite wordly, she may hesitate to show how she really feels lest he become impatient and unsympathetic. To have one's deep feelings ridiculed or considered unimportant is painful. It is like casting pearls before swine. If, however, a wife can say in her prayers, "Bless John as head of this family and give him the wisdom to guide us all in right ways," what strength it gives to a family. If a child says, "Bless daddy and mommy that they won't fight so much," how enlightening this is.

Frequently, couples sit and argue, never hearing or responding to the real meaning of the other's words or actions. In one dramatic session Brother and Sister E. became quite heated. She was bitterly denouncing his self-sufficiency, saying that he never needed her for anything except sex. As she raved on, the bishop noticed a tear forming in Brother E.'s eye. He let Sister E. go for sometime, and then he asked her if she knew her husband was crying. It so shocked her that she was speechless. The bishop then pointed to this as an example that they did not really listen to each other. He sent them home with instructions to listen and verify their impressions. By the next interview the E.'s were closer than they had ever been. After many months they were enjoying each other as never before.

In the intense relationship of marriage, partners cannot afford to neglect communication or take it for granted. One sister came storming into the bishop's office dragging behind her a bewildered husband. She said, "We had a terrible argument today!" Her husband agreed. The bishop asked what it was about. The husband didn't really know. He said that as soon as he walked in the door she started in. As the bishop inquired further, he discovered that Sister S. had been standing at the sink doing dishes and day dreaming. She remembered some past problems and began to think of what her husband had said. It made her angry to recall his remarks, so she began mentally reviewing appropriate come-backs. Soon she was engaged in a full-scale argument in her head. About that time, unsuspecting Brother S. walked through the door, and his complete amazement got hit with the results of his wife's day dreaming.

This happens nearly every day in every marriage. Each day dad lives in a different world than mother does, so that by the time he returns home they are on different wave lengths. Unless they develop a mutually acceptable way to reach out and rediscover each other, they will fail to communicate. Some couples do it by humor, such as posting a storm warning if things have gone poorly. Others frankly say "things were rotten today, so steer clear until sanity returns." Too many, though, express their misery in a contest to say whose day was worse, and neither spouse hears the other. Effective communication is one key to a healthy marriage. Its importance cannot be overestimated.

A problem that sometimes creates friction and irritation in families is that a wife who is a strong, agressive person cannot let her husband be head of the family. Perhaps he married her because he was unsure of himself and she gave him a feeling of security. There is nothing wrong with this if the wife still respects her husband as head of the family and encourages him to take the lead.

Sometimes a very spiritual girl will marry a man who is not so zealous in the Church. Although he is a good man and a loving husband and father, he has not yet acquired much spiritual depth. Success in business is so important that it occupies most of his time and thoughts. How can she view him as a patriarch standing at the head of her family when she is so far ahead of him spiritually?

The answer lies in the fact that the Lord loves this man and knows he has a great potential. Therefore he blessed him with a good, strong wife who could stand by patiently, encouraging and supporting him until he progresses to her spiritual level. Then they can go forward together. If she becomes impatient and nags, if she overpowers him and makes him feel inferior, if she assumes it is her job to teach him how to be a patriarch in the home, she may easily wreck this marriage or drive her husband into inactivity. A man learns how to be a patriarch in priesthood meetings. Problems and questions should be taken to his priesthood quorum leader or to the bishop. These, of course, can and should be discussed with his wife, but it is not her place to teach him his responsibilities. This falls to the men who are the priesthood authorities over him.

Some women also resent the fact that the man has the priesthood and that they are relegated to what they feel is an inferior station.

Why should God give His sons a power that is denied His daughters? Should they not be equal in His sight as to status and opportunity to perform the labors of life? Since women are just as necessary in life as are men (indeed life were impossible without them), justice demands their recognition before their Father in Heaven. Surely, a just God can have no favorites!

This division of responsibility is for a wise and noble purpose. Our Father in Heaven has bestowed upon His daughters a gift of equal importance and power, which gift, if exercised in its fulness, will occupy their entire life on earth so that they can have no possible longing for that which they do not possess. The "gift" referred to is that of motherhood—the noblest, most soul-satisfying of all earthly experiences. If this power is exercised righteously, woman has no time nor desire for anything greater, for there is nothing greater on earth! This does not mean that women may not use to the full their special gifts, for they are possessed of human free agency to the same extent as are men. Also, the more woman exercises her innate qualifications the greater is her power for motherhood. Woman may claim other activity, but motherhood should take precedence in her entire scheme of life.

The gift and responsibilities of motherhood make it desirable that women should be freed from the obligations of active service in the Priesthood. A fair and wise adjustment has been made by the Lord, so that women may have the freedom from unnecessary Church responsibility in order to magnify their great calling as mothers of men. (*Priesthood and Church Government,* p. 84.)

Unfortunately, motherhood and homemaking have been downgraded in the modern world. Many women feel useless if they are "only a housewife." This is not the design of the Lord, who sees men and women as equals, each with his own unique function and responsibilities.

In some cases it is the man who becomes enamored with the idea of priesthood authority and makes his wife feel inferior. Brother Widstoe clarifies this.

The possession of the Priesthood and its consequent family leadership should make men very considerate of woman. The man who arrogantly feels that he is better than his wife because he holds the Priesthood, has failed utterly to comprehend the meaning and purpose of Priesthood. He needs to remember that the Lord loves His daughters quite as well as His sons. It is but a small and puny souled man who could wish to humiliate women as a class and keep them as an inferior sex; for men can never rise superior to the women who bear and nurture them. (*Priesthood and Church Government,* p. 89.)

Respect is a key word between husband and wife—respect and appreciation. A woman needs to be told that she is loved and that what she does in the home is valued and appreciated. A man needs to be told that he is the greatest ever in the eyes of his wife and that she truly values all the hard work he puts in to support her and the children.

Another possible area of incompatibility in marriage is the sexual relationship. Trouble here is often a symptom of problems in other areas, but sometimes misunderstandings begin on the wedding night. A man may seek his own pleasures without regard for the physical and emotional delicacy of his wife. In a self-controlled courtship period the most intimate act has been a passionate embrace and kiss. Even in those many courtships that go beyond self-control but stop short of sexual intercourse, the woman is not prepared for the intensity of complete sexual communion. Thus, if the excited husband satisfies his drives, whatever the cost, his wife is hurt physically and emotionally, and the scars remain unless strong healing measures are taken.

One couple, the R.'s, seem to represent many. She was twenty-four and he twenty-eight. They had been through seminary and high school together. They came from a small Utah community and she had waited for him while he served as a missionary. Upon his return, they were married in the temple. The preparations leading to and including the ceremony and reception were ideal. Then he took his fresh, sweet bride home, and they began to express their love, unfettered by previous restrictions. As is often the case, his passion—though not greater than hers—developed more rapidly. He initiated and completed his part of sexual intercourse in about ten minutes from the time they went to bed. It was their first experience, so in addition to being strange, it hurt her physically. Her husband failed to realize this. He did not know that his climax came much faster than hers. He did not consider that to her intercourse was an expression of love, while he, frankly, did not really see it as much other than a very pleasurable experience. So, in his blind self-indulgence, he submitted his wife to pain and frustration for the first few weeks of marriage until her brain was programmed to regard sex as repulsive and painful. However, in that long-suffering way of women she endured this for years until it became unbearable. Then she began refusing his advances, which quickly produced a high degree of tension in the marriage.

Fortunately they turned to their wise bishop, who interviewed them separately, got the facts, and then helped them to talk it over in three or four interviews. He did not lecture them but gave them a reputable book which explained the facts about the human body. He also had Brother R. read the scriptures where Paul gave excellent marriage counsel.

> Wives, submit yourselves unto your own husbands, as unto the Lord.
> For the husband is the head of the wife, even as Christ is the head of the church: and he is the saviour of the body.
> Therefore, as the church is subject unto Christ, so let the wives be to their own husbands in every thing.
> Husbands, love your wives, even as Christ also loved the church, and gave himself for it; . . . .
> So ought men to love their wives as their own bodies. He that loveth his wife loveth himself.
> For no man ever yet hated his own flesh; but nourisheth and cherisheth it, even as the Lord the church. . . .
> For this cause shall a man leave his father and mother and shall be joined unto his wife, and they two shall be one flesh. . . .
> Nevertheless let every one of you in particular so love his wife even as himself; and the wife see that she reverence her husband. (Eph. 22-25, 28, 29, 31, 33.)

Now, Brother R. did not need extensive therapy. What he really needed was to be tender and kind toward his wife, making the sexual act an expression of the respect as well as the passion he felt for her. She had deep, untapped reservoirs of feelings that surprised him. Eventually the wounds healed. It is not always this easy, but often the maladjustments of marriage can be corrected with communication or prevented early in the marriage by tenderness **and consideration.**

Regarding sex, it is at this stage that the value of chastity is strongly borne out. It is impossible to overestimate the confidence that one feels knowing that his or her spouse exercised self-control before they met. There are many stressful situations which occur throughout marriage, the outcome of which depends upon the trust the couple has in each other.

Sometimes the problems of people in all aspects of living become so complicated and the immaturities left over from childhood render them so ineffectual that the individual is pushed into what is commonly called mental illness. Within the context of this discussion, this means that the programming of the mortal brain has been so out of harmony with the premortal learning of the spirit that the two are having difficulty existing together. If the spirit becomes so confused and weakened that the real world becomes unmanageable, he may slip into the unreal world that is safer and less painful. It is really a sickness of the spirit.

Mental illness is, of course, an exceedingly complex subject about which there are many theories. However, it is generally recognized that there is no sharp dividing line between the sick and the well person. Almost everyone contains within himself weaknesses which under enough stress could cause a breakdown.

In mental illness, many factors contribute to the problem. Love of self—or lack of it—is extremely important, as is the love of others. Those who should have been close to a person—his family, his friends—have for some reason not filled his spiritual and emotional needs. Sometimes the person himself has been so damaged in childhood that he shuts out those who would help him. He is unable to give or receive love. Long and patient reprogramming is necessary to overcome this handicap. Most people do not have the time or patience to give the enormous amount of love and emotional support needed by such a person, so he continues to feel rejected.

Love is not enough, however. The person himself must also make an effort to grow. This brings him to the three principles previously mentioned: (1) he needs a knowledge of the laws of God, which are a blue print for successful and happy living; (2) he must have a desire to do something about his problems. (The love and confidence of others can help to motivate this. Faith is powerful.); and (3) through continuing effort he must slowly build the power to control his life. The spirit has literally lost control. The appetites and passions of the body, emotions, and other people govern behavior. No wonder the spirit is sick! Free agency has been nullifiied. The time required to heal this kind of illness will depend upon the depth of the deprivation and the weakness of the spirit.

Brother C. was so convinced he was unworthy that he asked the bishop to remove his name from the Church records. He seemed so agitated that the bishop referred him to a professional counselor for diagnosis.

Brother C. and his older sister were reared in Phoenix, Arizona, by distant relatives, as their parents had divorced when Brother C. was five years of age. There were shuffled from relative to relative until he was seventeen, when he left home. His sister had left the previous year.

His relatives were not members of the Church, so when brother C. left home he had not been taught any gospel principles. After working at several odd jobs he joined the Marines and was stationed in the southern United States, where he became excessively immoral. He engaged in heavy drinking, petty thievery, and sexual promiscuity. This pattern continued until he met some Latter-day Saint servicemen whose example and association eventually re-activated him in the Church. He became so active that he began studying long hours preparing for a mission after his service. This pace of studying too hard eventually caught up with him and he had a nervous breakdown. The Marine psychiatrists were unable to help him so he was discharged. He leveled off after discharge and met a non-Latter-day Saint girl whom he married. She later joined the Church and they were sealed in the temple and had two children.

Brother C. rose rapidly in his employment due to his quick mind and hard work, but with each promotion he felt more pressure, especially since he felt handicapped without a high school diploma. He was felt handicapped without a high school diploma. He was called to the MIA superintendency, where he observed the youth of his ward and compared them to himself, thinking of himself as unclean.

Eventually he had a second nervous breakdown and went to his bishop asking for his name to be removed from the Church records.

Brother C. was a tall, very handsome, athletic type of man. His wife was very petite and pretty. They made an impressive looking couple, but inside they were both extremely insecure. As Brother C.'s story unfolded, two major factors became obvious. One was that he did not understand the gospel, especially the principle of repentance. The other fact was that he had little, if any, comprehension of how to be a husband, father, or patriarch. Because his childhood was so lacking in parental guidance and religious training, he grew up never seeing how an active Latter-day Saint man behaved. By the time he was twelve his ideas about men were largely formed. Soon after that he was in the service, where many men seem totally coarse and immoral. Then, when he became active again, he failed to learn thoroughly about repentance, so that as he learned more of the gospel, especially temple marriage, he began to feel unclean to the point of complete unworthiness. This so depressed him that he became convinced he should leave the Church. He even attempted suicide. His load of guilt was unbearable. Two factors became evident, both related to love and sex.

Brother C. could not rid himself of his feelings about having had promiscuous sexual relations. Although he had confessed this to his bishop upon baptism, what he did not tell the bishop was that he occasionally remembered those times with some pleasure. In discussion with the counselor he came to see that he had experienced relationships which gave him security in his lonely childhood, even though it was immoral to do so in a sexual way. What Brother C. was remembering with pleasure was that feeling of security, not the sex act. The other aspect was that Brother C. had never really experienced love in childhood except in this distorted way. Therefore, today as an adult, he could not experience it in a relaxed healthy way with his wife. He could not even imagine that his bishop could love him, let alone his Heavenly Father. This, in turn, affected how he treated his wife and children.

The bishop, using the counselor's evaluation, undertook a three-pronged approach. First, he assigned the elders quorum president to Brother C. as a home teaching companion. He told this man that Brother C. needed to observe a Latter-day Saint patriarch in action in all phases of life. Soon their families were sharing outings and home evenings and the men were sharing do-it-yourself projects and priesthood activities. An important factor, though, was that before this began, *both* Brother C. and his elders quorum president understood its purpose. This permitted the president to be more specific than ordinary acquaintance normally permits.

The second step was to teach Brother C. the gospel. This was done through actual tutoring by a stake missionary. This man, a seventy, was experienced in life in addition to his outstanding gospel knowledge, so he helped Brother C. relearn the gospel, especially from the standpoint of love and repentance.

The third step involved permitting Brother C. to *earn* his peace of mind. He **was convinced** that for him to take his family to the celestial kingdom would be very difficult. So, the bishop, as moved by the Spirit, agreed in large measure and told Brother C. that he must begin to *work* out his salvation. He needed to make restitution in some way for his wrongdoings. Only then would he be able to feel that he was forgiven and so erase his guilt feelings. From then on Brother C. was very active in that ward. Being careful not to endanger his family or health, the bishop helped him to earn his salvation by constant, demanding service in the kingdom. The more he worked, the closer he became to his Father in heaven, to his family, and to himself.

After two years of steady improvement Brother C. was a changed man. He had never been more secure and happy. He had learned about repentance and forgiveness first hand. He had learned how to be a husband and father in the finest Latter-day Saint tradition. Through his labors he had learned to serve people in the spirit of love and could understand how his colleagues and his Father in heaven could love him. He was not finished and had many battles ahead, but now he had the equipment to fight those battles. Paul, in words which apply to the mentally ill and their struggles to regain health, speaks of charity or love.

> For now we see through a glass, darkly; but then face to face: now I know in part; but then shall I know even as also I am known.
> And now abideth faith, hope, charity, these three; but the greatest of these is charity. (1 Cor. 13:12-12.)

This charity or love had been given generously, by Brother C.'s bishop, his home teaching companion, a stake missionary, and his wife.

Part of the cure for mental illness lies in the principle of honesty. This is often hard to come by in human relations. Many, if not most, human conflicts would cease if the antagonist were honest with each other and with themselves. Many so-called progressives today advocate a perverted form of honesty as they sponsor nude therapy, confrontation groups, free speech (meaning license), the living theater, ad nauseam. They cloud the real issue of honesty.

It is true that nearly everyone generally deceives himself and others by fear, inhibitions, and defensiveness. To hide from the truth is a destructive course. Joseph Smith considered this to be a step toward apostasy and spiritual decay.

> Because their hearts are set so much upon the things of this world, and aspire to the honors of men, that they do not learn this one lesson—
>
> That the rights of the priesthood are inseparably connected with the powers of heaven, and that the powers of heaven cannot be controlled nor handled only upon the principles of righteousness.
>
> That they may be conferred upon us, it is true; *but when we undertake to cover our sins, or to gratify our pride, our vain ambition, or to exercise control or dominion or compulsion upon the souls of the children of men,* in any degree of unrighteousness, behold, the heavens withdraw themselves; the Spirit of the Lord is grieved; and when it is withdrawn, Amen to the priesthood or the authority of that man. (D&C 121:35-37; italics added.)

Honesty and forthrightness are hallmarks of the gospel and evidences of a stable, healthy person. People who appropriately admit their failings cannot be ensnared by the pressures of keeping up appearances. As they are honest about their job, their ambitions, their capacities, they will not spend money to keep up with the Joneses and then be depressed by their bills. They will not inveigle their way into social entanglements that put pressure on them to compete and to pose. They will not take civic or other volunteer assignments that exceed their capacity to deliver.

Honesty tends to breed a sense of humor, for what honest man cannot help but laugh at himself much of the time?

So the mature person moves into a rather well-earned part of life in which many of the battles are over and in which he can consolidate his gains, spiritual and temporal.

It was no easy path, and to even arrive at this point is a great accomplishment.

Chapter 10
The Later Years
Enduring (and Growing) to the End

Chapter 10

Enduring (and Growing) to the End

Aging is a lifelong process that begins at birth. As the years roll on, the relationship between the eternal spirit and the body changes somewhat because the body is slowly deteriorating. The spirit may still feel young and strong, but the body no longer responds quickly and easily to its demands. This is disconcerting. As has been stated, the body needs to be vigorous and in good condition for the spirit to operate at maximum efficiency. Most young people do not give much thought to the care of the body because it is working automatically and gives them little trouble. Even when it is abused it adjusts quickly.

Older people know that this situation does not last forever. Health and vitality are valued most when one begins to lose them. Hypochondriacs abound among the aged partly because of concern for their health and partly because their spiritual and mental progress may be slowed or stopped. With nothing to do, boredom leads to stagnation.

Often, retirement is anticipated as a time of freedom

from responsibility and pressure so that the individual has twenty-four hours a day to think of nothing but pleasure and recreation. He lets down completely, thinking this is what will make him happy.

The laws of God, however, are still in operation. A person who is not progressing will be unhappy. For older people, however, progress can take different forms. More sedentary, less demanding pursuits can be found. If Brother Jones wakes up morning after morning with no obligations, nothing he really *must* do besides eating and just existing, then he himself must impose some challenging activities that will keep him mentally alert, give him physical exercise, and keep his spirit interested in life. This becomes more and more difficult. Some people give up and stop trying. Sometimes inactivity is forced upon a person due to illness and indisposition of the body. To keep physically fit, mentally alert, and spiritually strong are the particular challenges of the later years. Society and often even families do not help much with this.

In the modern world there is a tendency to separate all the people into age groups. There are the preschoolers, the school age children, the teenagers, the young marrieds, the middle aged, the retirement set, and the aged. People who do this are thinking mostly in terms of the body. According to this, small children are inferior, teenagers and young marrieds are the most important and valuable, the middle aged are going downhill, and old people are almost completely useless.

This is a pernicious, untrue, misleading doctrine. Taking into account the spirit and its eternal progression, every age is a good age and should be valued equally. As has been indicated, unity in a family requires that the members relate horizontally, not vertically. This includes grandma and grandpa. Activities which include all age groups are valuable in fostering understanding and communication between them. *Every* age has its own particular problems and challenges. People of every age need the help and support of other people.

Progression is often difficult for older individuals because most of them have been sidetracked from the mainstream of society. Many are put away somewhere to vegetate until they die. This is cruel and unfeeling. It shows a lack of insight into the needs of every human soul. The body does deteriorate, but the spirit can continue to grow, especially in wisdom, insight, and harmony with the spirit of God.

Besides the need to grow, everyone, regardless of age, also needs to love and to be loved, to be respected and valued as a human being, and to feel adequate to handle life situations. These, too, are often denied the old people in today's world. Their free agency is often disregarded. As the body ages a person does become less capable in some ways, but this does not mean that he is less valuable as a person or that he should not be respected. He needs even more love, kindness, and understanding.

Many old people are sent to rest homes because their children do not want to assume the responsibility for their care. Some go to retirement colonies by their own choice because they no longer feel needed or even comfortable with younger people, who scorn them. They do not want to feel dependent.

To be isolated from those you love or to be considered a useless burden is cruel. In the patriarchal order, grandfather is still the senior priesthood authority and should be respected as such. His opinions and ideas should be given careful consideration as long as his brain is sound. This is important for his mental health.

Many young people tend to think that everything new is better and everything old is out-of-date and old fashioned, hence worthless. This, too, is a false doctrine. There are some things that never change and will always be true. Human personality has been the same in all periods of time and in all cultures. The laws regulating this are the same today as they were two thousand years ago when Jesus walked the dusty roads of Palestine. They were the same in the times of Abraham, Noah, and Adam. They were probably the same on other worlds where the spirit children of God lived for a few thousand years, then passed on to higher spheres.

In today's world science has taken the place of God as a final authority. Since the scientist is not concerned about good and bad, right and wrong, but only about reporting what he finds, the old moral code has been thrown out and nothing has been put in its place. The wisdom of the ages has too often been abandoned simply because it is old and not measurable scientifically.

By the young, parents may be considered hopelessly old fashioned. Grandparents, they think, are an anachronism left over from some previous period of time totally unrelated to the modern, fast-moving world. The gospel of Jesus Christ teaches different concepts, but that is old too.

The crucial question is whether or not young people have a personal testimony that God lives and that Jesus Christ is who he says he is. If they know that God lives and that he really did create this world in all its marvelous complexity, then they can believe that what he says is true. To create this world God would have to have known and understood every single scientific law governing every phase of existence. That means that he is a long, long way ahead of any scientists who have ever lived upon this earth. He not only knows more, but he has combined this with a completely moral and ethical nature. God is *good*. He is *loving*. His work and glory is to bring to pass the immortality and eternal life of his children. Therefore he will never tell them anything that is not true or that will hurt them. *Every statement of Jesus Christ is true and is given for the welfare of the people of this earth.* That is the one irrefutable fact that must be accepted by those who believe in God, whatever their age.

Older people in The Church of Jesus Christ of Latter-day Saints are probably respected and valued more than in any other group. Opportunities within the Church for service are manifold. Priesthood activities, the welfare program, Relief Society work, genealogy, and teaching are all areas in which older people can function according to their abilities and interests.

Every consideration should be given to them, as well as to every member of the family. At every age there are developmental tasks to be achieved and there are challenges and problems which make growth difficult. This is necessary, however, as growth requires *effort*. People therefore need other people to encourage and sustain them while they are struggling with their own particular set of problems.

In the Book of Mormon, we read how Alma was about to baptize a group of people. In preparing them for this he said,

> ". . . and now, as ye are desirous to come into the fold of God, and to be called his people, and are willing to bear one another's burdens, that they may be light;
> Yea, and are willing to mourn with those that mourn; yea, and comfort those that stand in need of comfort, and to stand as witnesses of God at all times and in all things, and in all places that ye may be in. . .
> . . . if this be the desire of your hearts, what have you against being baptized. . . ." (Mosiah 18:8-10.)

All Latter-day Saints, as part of their covenant with God, agree to help and comfort other people, and especially other Church members, regardless of age or other considerations. Obeying the commandments of God includes sharing and caring; it includes *loving* in the broad and deep sense of the word.

To be aware of and to be willing to help carry the responsibility for the needs of older people—physical, mental, and spiritual—is part of the gospel of Jesus Christ. Also, within the patriarchal order children are *obligated* to care for their aging parents. These spirits may still be feeling vital and young. They sacrificed to bring children into the world and to care for them. Loving children should welcome the opportunity to be of service to parents and to grandparents.

Before the Millenium the Saints are supposed to come to a unity of the faith. This means that all people need to learn to give and receive. They must give of themselves for the benefit of others. People in need should be able to accept help without feeling inferior. The whole body of the Church will have to achieve a harmony so that the words of the Savior may be a reality: "Let them be one, Father, even as thou and I are one."

This is not only a general truth but a specific law of family life. Family activities which include everyone, even grandma and grandpa, are important so that all members can get this feeling of unity and sharing. Children should be taught to watch for ways in which they can be helpful. They should know that other people need them as much as they need their families. Old people also need to show patience and consideration for others in the family. As long as they can they should carry the responsibility for their own welfare and take care of themselves. Most of them want to do this.

The message of this chapter is that old people are as important as anyone else and should be respected and given the help they need so that they can live out their lives in dignity and comfort. Family and Church unity are essential. Faith in God is basic.

Epilogue

As the eternal progression of man started in the premortal world and continued in mortality so will it continue on into the life to come. The blending of a spirit with a body was a most crucial step in this progression. Mortal life is the place where the spirit learns to control the body and to live in harmony with it. This is the place where men can, by becoming followers of Jesus Christ, be initiated into the great organization of the government of God by receiving the priesthood. In this world men and women, joined together in holy matrimony by those holding priesthood authority and sealed by the Holy Spirit of Promise, can learn to blend their lives into a smooth functioning team—one in spirit, one in purpose—to go on into the eternities as a family unit in the Kingdom of God. Each generation in this earth provides bodies for spirits who are to follow in the next generation. They murture, protect, and teach these spirits until they achieve manhood and womanhood so that they can go on, first by themselves, later with their chosen mates.

Latter-day Saint parents have been given the great responsibility of helping to raise up a righteous race of people. It is a great and noble calling which must be accomplished in a world ruled by Satan. The Father's choice spirits have been saved to be born in the last days so that they would be strong enough to combat the evil and triumph in the Lord's work.

This can be accomplished by wise, intelligent, and strong application of eternal truth. It is not chance or luck or fate.

The truth actually shall make men free.

Index

Adam and Eve, 120
Aging, 161

Belonging, 107
Brain, 14

Cain, 61
Chastity, 78, 151
Church, programs, 5; resources offered by, 67, 100
Communication, 143, 144; within marriages, 143
Competition, 88
Computers, 14
Cooperation, 53
Culture, defined, 7

Discipline, 62, 95

Education, 82
Emotions, 60
Erikson, Erik, 35
Eternal procreation, 76
Eternal progression, 52, 109
Evil spirits, 16

Faith, 35, 52, 83
Finances, 136
Fore-ordained, 12
Free agency, 45, 56, 120

Grandparents, 164
Greenspun, Hank, 109
Growth, not smooth, 71

Honesty, 156
Human dignity, 112

Integrity, 107, 118
Intelligence, 79, 82

Language, 51
Leisure time, 114
Love, 124; defined, 24; a key to mental health, 26; mature, 126

Marriages, problems in, 135
Mental illness, 151
Mind, defined, 15
Modesty, 78

Moral code, 95
Motherhood, 43, 148
Mothers, working, 5

McKay, David O., 5, 28

Naaman, 5
Nicknames, 110

Obedience, 54
Older people, in the Church, 164

Parable of the talents, 90
Parents, become models, 73
Patriarchal order, 138
Perversion, 30
Power to control, 123
Prayer, 64, 65
Premortal education, 13
Premortal state, 11
Priesthood, 148
Priesthood authority, 138
Prisoners of war, 24
Progression, 163
Punishment, 97

Repentance, 52, 97, 98, 99, 124
Respect, 112, 148
Responsibility, 113, 115
Retirement, 161
Revelation, parents entitled to, 66
Self-control, 28, 59
Sense of identity, 106
Sex, 7, 78, 151
Sex education, 77, 78
Sex instruction, 100
Sexual attitudes, 73
Sexual maturity, 110
Skills, 91
Smith, Joseph, 15, 16
Success, 42
Successful marriages, 135

Unity, 62, 63, 130, 138

Widstoe, John A., 148
Will to obey, 123
Work, 114

Young, Brigham, 42